The Greening of Christian Education

The Greening of Christian Education

Brian V. Hill

Professor of Education
Murdoch University
Western Australia

LANCER

Lancer Books
3–5 Richmond Road
Homebush West, NSW, Australia

National Library of Australia
Cataloguing-in-Publication Data

Hill, Brian V. 1934 —
The greening of Christian education.

Bibliography.
ISBN 0 85892 253 3

1. Christian education. I. Title.

207

Typeset and Printed in Singapore
by Singapore National Printers (Pte) Ltd.

A PSALM

Unless the sap of God's Spirit
rise within me,
I am a dead leaf.
I have no root in myself.
Lapsed from the stem of salvation
I drift on the parching wind.
I cherish the branch from which
my soul has budded.
Green me well, O Lord.

Contents

Preface 11

A. **TEACHING IN YESTERDAY'S CHURCH** 13

1 **Christian Education in Hiatus** 15

2 **The Teacher in Earlier Times** 21

Teaching in the Old Testament (22) — Schools and Sophists in Greek Times (26) — Teaching in the New Testament (30) — Schools and Clerics in the Middle Ages (32)

3 **The Rise of Schooled Societies** 38

Schools and Teachers in the Reformation (39) — Schools for the Industrial Society (42) — The Sunday School Movement (45) — The Deschooling Critique (48) — Compulsion, Learning and Commitment (51) — Schools and Social Control (54)

4 **The Modern Concept of Education** 59

Secularisation (60) — The Scope of Education (64) — The Concept of Christian Education (68) —

Indoctrination and Evangelism (72) — Christian Nurture (75) — What Point Have We Reached? (80)

B. TEACHING IN TODAY'S CHURCH 83

5 Teaching for Commitment 85

Changing Commitment (86) — Teaching and Commitment (88) — The Curriculum Process (92) — Relevance to Christian Teaching (97)

6 Specifying Learning Objectives 102

A General Aim (102) — Developmental Factors (104) — Framing Objectives Statements (105) — Needs-Assessment (107) — The Scope of Our Aim (110) — About the Examples (111)

7 Content: Bible and Life 124

Changing Subject Matter (124) — States of Mind in Bible Readers (129) — Summary (133) — Excursus on Hermeneutics (134) — Biblical Heritage and Contemporary Experience (137) — Biblical Truth and Contemporary Application (140)

8 Learning Environments and Resources 145

The Home (146) — The Church: Its Forms of Life (151) — The Church: Appropriate Learning Environments (156) — The Mass Media and Entertainment Venues (163) — Outdoor Settings (165) — Learning Resources (166) — Furniture: The Hidden Agenda (167)

9 Guiding the Church's Teaching Programmes .. 172

One Body, Many Gifts (173) — Enabling Ministries (177) — Administrative Structures (179) — An Administrative Lattice (189) — Core Curriculum (194) — The Church Calendar (197) — Epilogue (198)

Select Bibliography 201

ABBREVIATIONS

JCE	Journal of Christian Education
JET	Journal of Educational Thought
NT	New Testament
OT	Old Testament
Them	Themelios

Tables

Diagram 5.1	The Curriculum Process	93
Diagram 5.2	A Curriculum Model for Teaching in the Church	100
Diagram 6.1	A Check-List for Evaluating Objectives Statements	112
Example 1	A Sample Adult Needs-Assessment Questionnaire	113
Example 2	Report of a Youth Needs Enquiry	119
Example 3	Objectives of a Christian Education Course	121
Example 4	Objectives for a Self-esteem Workshop	122
Diagram 7.1	Possible States of Mind When Approaching the Bible	130
Diagram 7.2	Stages in Interpreting the Bible	136
Diagram 7.3	Biblical Truth and Contemporary Application	141
Diagram 8.1	Check-List for Evaluating Curriculum Resources	168

Diagram 8.2 A Minimal Equipment List 169

Diagram 9.1 The Gifts of the Spirit 175

Diagram 9.2 A Clerical-Star System 181

Diagram 9.3 A Clerical-Support System 185

Diagram 9.4 A Congregational-Support System 187

Diagram 9.5 A Body-Life Support System 190

Preface

In 1970, with the disturbances of the 'sixties still fresh in memory, an author named Charles A. Reich wrote a book called *The Greening of America*. His thesis was that American society had become locked into the dehumanising mind-set of the corporate state. This mind-set or Consciousness II was characterised by a false perception of values and satisfactions, thinking itself happy to be manipulated by consumerist business and big government. But Consciousness II, said Reich, was about to self-destruct. Amongst the new generation of bright young people, Consciousness III was beginning to emerge. Liberated from conformity, materialism and the competitive spirit, they were the beautiful people, back to nature in jeans and beads, out into new paths of the spirit on mind-expanding drugs. Society was about to change fundamentally.

Little more than a decade later, Reich's book reads like a fairy tale from some past romantic era. His new generation seems to have been a transient cultural wave whipped up by the passions of the Vietnam conscription period and then repressed by the weight of economic recession. Reich foretold a golden age of self-expression ushered in by the conversion of the members of society to Consciousness III. But since he was not using the term in the Christian sense of a renewal of the heart and mind and a turning to God, his golden age proved to be just a mirage.

Yet I am cautiously optimistic that a greening of another kind may in fact be on the way. It seems to me that there is a stirring amongst Christians which points the way to freer forms of congregational life, with the focus on the ministries of all rather than the role of the ordained minister, and on dynamic patterns of fellowship rather than upon staid formality in worship. I sense an awakening of spiritual gifts amongst the people as a whole which is beginning to release more resources than the institutional church has tapped for centuries. And in this movement of God, if that is what it is, the gifts of teaching and training will play a crucial part.

Thoughts of this kind, which had been gathering strength over some time, were provided with an outlet when I was invited by my good friend Dr. Noel Vose, principal of the Baptist Theological College of Western Australia, to re-design and teach a course in that college on 'Christian Education'. This book has grown out of that experience.

I am grateful to Noel and his colleagues Drs. Richard Moore and John Olley for their encouragement and interest in the result. John in particular found time to contribute detailed and very helpful comments on the first draft. The student group also helped to keep my feet on the ground — in class. They can't answer for the book!

At a further remove, I was also helped by the keen criticisms of Dr. Peter Hill, Christian friend and research officer in the state Education Department. My wife Margaret was as ever a patient and perceptive sounding board, while Freida Giblett did wonders in transferring my scribble to script. I can safely attribute to all these good friends a deep concern for the teaching ministries of the Christian faith community. To this cause I dedicate whatever insights this book has disclosed.

Brian V. Hill,
Murdoch University,
Western Australia.

Part A

TEACHING IN YESTERDAY'S CHURCH

1

Christian Education in Hiatus

The phrase 'Christian education' does not appear in the Bible. Perhaps this should warn us that the imposing range of services provided by churches and denominations in the name of Christian education may possibly be more culturally conditioned than biblically commanded. This becomes clearer when we consider some of the activities to which the label is attached.

Some use the term when speaking of the teaching of religion in the public school.[1] Others use it for classes in Christian belief, as distinct from classes in religious studies, in church schools. Yet others use it to encompass the whole curriculum of a 'Christian school'. Another range of uses comes into operation within church groups and denominations. Thus 'departments of Christian education' offer training facilities for Christian evangelists, teachers and pastoral workers. And the traditional Sunday School is understood to provide Christian education for the children of the faithful and in some all-age Sunday school patterns for the adults as well.

Thirteen years ago in a previous book, I pleaded for a moratorium on the use of the term 'Christian education' until we had subjected each of the various structures involved to critique, and had clarified what we thought we were doing in each case.[2] But little has changed in either terminology or practice. In the meantime, increasing hiatus is evident in virtually every area of

Christian teaching effort. And unfortunately, Christian leaders tend to respond to pressures in a defensive way which lacks a thought-out rationale. They often appear to be more concerned with preserving whatever remnants of a Christian monopoly remain in the culture than in asking whether their attitudes are in fact Christian and biblical.

Thus, for example, the hiatus in public school religious instruction has been made worse by conflicting Christian views of what should actually happen in this area. Some Christians urge that we should use whatever political muscle we have left to keep the monopoly of Christian beliefs and values intact, either by defining general religious instruction as Christian (Queensland) or by retaining the 'right of entry' for denominational representatives under a 'special religious instruction' clause (New South Wales). Conflicts within Christian ranks have left the way open for secular humanists in Victoria and Tasmania to achieve the complete exclusion of religious studies from the general curriculum.

One response to this hiatus has been to withdraw from the public school and establish more private Christian schools. In some, an initial motivation has been to ensure that Christianity was not left out of religious studies; indeed, to restore its monopoly. But there has also been a more substantial theoretical base for many such experiments, anchored in either Catholic or Presbyterian-Reformed convictions that the whole curriculum must be taught from a distinctively Christian perspective. Even here there is a growing hiatus. The Catholic and Reformed thought-systems differ radically at several points on what constitutes Christian education. Moreover, many Christians today are questioning the validity of the Christian school concept itself, and advocate other options such as Christian support and defence of the public schools or the formation of alternative public schools sponsored by local communities.

At least in one area, however, it might appear that the concept of Christian education is clearly understood and rightly applied. This is with respect to the teaching ministries of the gathered church, the community of committed believers. Here at least we seem to be on safe ground in speaking of programmes of

Christian education, through Sunday schools and other kinds of study groups devoted to strengthening believers in the understanding and application of their faith.

On closer examination, however, there appears to be mounting unease in this area also. Many people suspect that the Sunday school pattern has yielded too readily to the secular model of public education with its formalised curricula and professionalised teachers. Has something been lost by our use of teacher-pupil models and the delegation of spiritual nurture to an age-graded educational agency? Does the substantial fall-out of students upon reaching the teen years, and the reluctance of most adults to participate in study programmes, suggest that our enthusiasm has been misplaced?

We are so locked in to certain ways of doing things that many of the questions raised above may strike the reader as downright heretical. It may help at this stage if I affirm that my intention is to subject current practices to biblical critique, not to disregard biblical principles. My contention will be that we have allowed certain cultural trends to draw us away from the Bible's representation of what our teaching ministries should be like. And I will be trying to chart the way back to the teaching faith of Jesus and the apostles.

Some indication of the direction of the argument may be given by commenting on the nature and extent of the commitment to Christian education in the USA, for Australia is coming increasingly under the influence of American models of church growth and nurture. Many Australian churches are in grave danger of trying to copy American models without appreciating the differences between the two cultures and the shortcomings that some Americans are detecting in their own methods.

Visitors to that country cannot fail to be impressed by the size and scale of its 'education industry'. In the world's most schooled society, it is possible to place oneself under classroom tutelage from the cradle to the grave. The idea that education depends upon formal schooling is so deeply etched on the mind that even study at college and university level is commonly described as 'going to school', though the school in this case may well be a high-level 'graduate school' in a prestigious university.

Not less imposing is what may by analogy be called the 'Christian education industry' in that country. Denominations have highly professionalised departments of Christian education marketing curriculum kits no less comprehensive and glamorous than those on the secular market. Individual churches frequently have their own staff managing Christian education, occasionally even by-passing the congregation to hire teachers from the community at large for their Sunday schools.

Another evidence of the church's commitment to a secular model of education is the degree to which the private provision of general education parallels state education. Not only do Christian schools represent a significant and growing proportion of the total number of institutions from kindergarten to secondary level, but there are Christian colleges and universities which make it possible for one to proceed to the highest levels of graduate study in any subject without emerging from the institutional canopy of Christian education. Within many of these establishments, fully academic departments of Christian education develop a wide range of disciplinary studies all purporting to be necessary for an understanding of Christian education, and each generating its own avenues of career development.

The outside observer is likely to be more than a little bemused. Is all this a natural and inevitable outcome of Christ's command to go and teach? If our Lord were to return as a man of the people today, would he be discouraged from exercising his lay gifts until he had graduated from college? Would he want to teach in a Christian school? Would he select his disciples only from amongst graduates of Christian colleges? Would any church hire him as its director of Christian education?

Such questions are, of course, facetious. If there were a second incarnation, Christ would come in a form appropriate to the cultural milieu of that time. Even so, there is still room for uneasiness. In view of the way he treated the ecclesiastical and bureaucratic structures of the first century, might he not just possibly identify with the 'deschoolers' of our era, rather than the schoolmen? Ought we not to be a little less reverent towards the ethos of formal education and a little less eager to baptise it into church practice?

The illustration highlights the point made previously. There is confusion — I have used the even harsher word hiatus — in the field of Christian education. This is made more serious by the fact that political pressures associated with such questions as the funding of private schools by the state and the introduction of new religious studies approaches, tend to obscure the deeper level of questioning the theology of what we are doing. How should we conceptualise Christian education in relation to the objectives of the advancing Kingdom of God? The phrase has become a powerful slogan which tempts us to transfer secular powers to the church, to substitute professionalism for the exercise of the gifts of the laity, and to degrade evangelism to the level of indoctrination.

In this book I will argue that the whole conceptual structure of education as society at large conceives it must be called into question by Christians concerned with the church's teaching mandate. Along with the word 'education', I will query current views of 'teaching' and 'schooling', arguing that we are too much influenced by the Greek legacy and by pressures in the industrial society, and too little conscious of the alternative patterns appropriate to a Judaeo-Christian value-system.

Chapters two to four seek to break the nexus which exists in the thinking of most people today between the modern notions of schooling and education, and the teaching ministries of the gathered church. I will make some reference in chapter four to the implications of this critique for theories of religious studies, general education and Christian schools, but since I have dealt with these issues at greater length elsewhere, I will not dwell on them here.[3]

The critique also has consequences for Christians who train to be professional teachers. But again, I have written much on these matters in other places, and will only touch on them here to illustrate the point.[4]

Primarily, this book is written for people working in the teaching ministries of the gathered church. Some are clergy, some professional teachers, but most of them are lay people in both senses. Nevertheless they possess spiritual gifts in the area of teaching which are too often slighted either by our not calling on them or by our trying to force them into a professionalised mould.

For such people, the second half of the book is devoted to the more positive task of reconstructing a Judaeo-Christian approach to the church's teaching ministries. It is an attempt to move closer to the biblical ideal of a community of believers learning together and sharing their gifts and insights. I will try to indicate some of the lessons we can learn from professional studies of human learning and curriculum development, while avoiding what I see as the snares of the Christian education industry.

The result, hopefully, is that we will continue to have faith in teaching, but not teaching as the world understands it — flanked by the concept of education on one side and the paraphernalia of professional schooling on the other — rather teaching as the Scriptures define it: a gift exercised voluntarily within the nurturing community of faith.

Footnotes

1. Queensland is the one state where the government has decreed that the content will be promotion of Christian beliefs and values, against the advice of the report it commissioned in 1971 and refused to make public.
2. B. V. Hill, *Called to Teach: The Christian Presence in Australian Education* (Sydney: Angus and Robertson, 1971) 107.
3. See my articles in the *JCE* notably my 'Religious Instruction — An Anachronism' 50 (1974) 35–45 and 'Is it Time We Deschooled Christianity?' 63 (1978) 5–21.
4. See *Faith at the Blackboard* (Grand Rapids: Eerdmans, 1982) and the Teacher Action Study Kits (TASKS) published by the Australian Teachers' Christian Fellowship (Sydney: ATCF).

2

The Teacher in Earlier Times

Now that teaching has become a highly trained profession, it would seem reasonable to expect a fair degree of consensus regarding the characteristics of a good teacher. In fact, however, there is a wide divergence among the experts. Some stress the *instructional* aspect, whereby information is accurately passed on to the learner. Others stress the *behavioural* aspect, whereby habits and skills are effectively implanted. Others again stress the *relational* aspect: the acquisition of social and interpersonal skills through interaction with the teacher as a person. Finally, some stress the *rational* aspect, whereby the ability to think critically and independently is encouraged by the teacher's own example of rational behaviour.

The type and quality of teaching behaviour in the educational profession vary greatly, depending not only on the training received but on the kind of person the individual teacher is trying to be. There are many models to choose from. But one thing they tend to have in common is the formalising of the teacher-pupil relationship and the systematising of what is taught and tested. The reasons for this are complex, and will require us to pass in quick review over some of the high points in the historical development of the concepts of teaching and schooling.

My reason for doing this will be to show how significant are the differences between the secular models of professional teaching now so familiar to us, and the biblical concept of the teacher. It is important to do this, for references to 'teaching' and such related terms as 'instruction' and 'training' abound in the Scriptures. In the present chapter I will touch on ideas of teaching in the Old Testament, the high culture of Greece, the New Testament, and the later Middle Ages. In chapter three I will pick up the story in the Reformation period, showing how the seeds of universal schooling were sown at this time and came to full flower later as a result of the pressures exerted by the Industrial Revolution.

Teaching in the Old Testament

Judaism introduces us to a teaching God. Our fallen race is seen to have lapsed into a great ignorance of God's purposes, hence the Bible constantly testifies to God's redemptive desire to teach us what is right, that we may then teach others also. When Moses is called by God to lead a nation and starts to plead ignorance, the Lord says 'I will teach you what to do' (Exod 4:12)[1]. After God has revealed at Sinai the features of the alternative life-style which his covenant people are to cultivate, he then commands Moses to teach this law to the people (24:12). They, in their turn, are firmly charged to teach it to their children (Deut 6:4–9; 11:19).

There is strong emphasis on teaching 'these words', for the holy life is not sustained merely by good feelings or sincere intentions, but by a rounded *understanding* of God's ways. In a fallen world there are many traps for the unwary, and the way to be wary is to be more *aware*, to have a heightened consciousness of the way of life revealed by God.

The emphasis on words, however, is not to be taken as implying mere verbalism. Many teaching aids were employed to engage the attention and add meaning. Notable landmarks were given instructive names. Monuments were erected to invite questions about their significance. At the crossing of the Jordan, Joshua told the people to take twelve stones from the exposed river bed and build a memorial cairn so that in the future when their children asked: 'What do these stones mean?' they would be able to recount the story of God's deliverance. (Josh 4:6).

Also, there were the great ritual events of the covenant community. Imagine the sense of drama built up on the Day of Atonement. In the valley is a colourful tented structure visible to all the tribes stationed in orderly array on the hill-slopes. The high priest is performing special rites in front of a massive furnace, before disappearing into the tent. Children's voices whisper 'What's he doing in there?' and parents reply by describing the enacted concept of atonement (Lev 16). The tabernacle was one huge teaching aid.

And God teaches in the context of relationship. At the heart of family life is the Passover ritual. At the first institution of this solemn rite, it was expected that the children would ask what these things meant, and again it would be the parents' responsibility to explain the ways of God (Exod 11:26; 13:8).

It is worth noting that these moments of instruction came in the normal course of life, not in classrooms. And they were embedded in family interactions. More than this, they were interwoven with the work-life of the people; learning and living occurred together. The three great religious festivals — Passover, Pentecost, and Tabernacles — correlated with events in the agricultural calendar: Passover with the beginning of the barley harvest, Pentecost with the wheat harvest, and the Feast of Tabernacles with the grape harvest.[2] Thanks for God's provision of our bodily needs was entwined with thanks for spiritual deliverance.

What, it may be asked, about the priests, prophets and wise men of Jewish history? Surely here we have examples of great teachers? Some, like Samuel, Elijah and Elisha even seem to have gathered disciples about them (1 Sam 10:10; 19:20; 2 Kgs 2:3–5; 4:38; 6:1). The answer is that usually their message was a call to return to the original revelation of the law and to exercise the mutual teaching responsibilities of a covenant community. The priests carried out rituals whose significance depended on the faithfulness with which family instruction was kept. Insofar as they had a teaching role it was in training other priests and adults to understand the ritual illustrations of God's law (Deut 31:10–13; 33:8–10).[3]

As for the prophets, many were not even called from priestly ranks, as witness Gideon taken from the threshing floor, and Amos the herdsman from Tekoa. The bearers of truth were not a professionalised fraternity. The 'sons of the prophets' who gathered round Elijah do not seem to have been a school in any effective sense, but rather an informal community of followers which did not outlive the master's successor, Elisha.

The third group of leaders with teaching functions was the 'wise men',[4] such as those who generated the Wisdom Literature of the Bible. Many ancient cultures developed collections of proverbs or wise sayings dealing with the practical affairs of life. What distinguished the biblical sages, who were probably well aware of such traditions in the Near East,[5] was the anchorage they found in the 'fear of the Lord'. Hence their teaching intimately bound together the spheres of religion, personal morality, business and social life. Their functions appear to have been related more to counselling leaders and lay folk on request than to training the young or developing systematic instruction. But they did much to reinforce the authority of God, who is both creator and deliverer, over the whole of life.

As all teachers know, the work must be done afresh with each new generation. But the teachers of Israel grew slack and the nation slipped into idolatry and division. There was a brief revival of the old values in the reign of Josiah, when renovators of the temple discovered a copy of the 'book of the law of the Lord.' In a rare moment of unanimity, a king, a high priest and a prophetess united to have the law read before a gathering of families and sealed with a revived enactment of the Passover ritual (2 Chr 34:14–35:19).

But this was an atypical event. The moral and spiritual slippage of the divided nation continued until conquest and exile emptied the promised land of covenant people. When remnants of the Israelite clans began to filter back into Palestine in the time of Ezra and Nehemiah, an urge developed to rebuild national identity on the foundation of systematic teaching. In a ceremony reminiscent of Josiah's reformation, Ezra the priest and scribe led the Jerusalem community in a great public reading of the law. At this time particular care was taken to give 'the meaning so that the people could understand what was being read' (Neh 8:8). For this purpose, teaching assistants were trained to instruct the people at large.

Out of this developed a profession of teachers and a pattern of schools. Judaism became and has remained a tradition of universal training in the knowledge of the law, or *torah*. The rabbis, or teaching scribes, displaced the sacrificing priests as the leaders of the faithful; a process completed some time in the first century of the Christian era.[6] Synagogues, places of meeting in which the reading of the *torah* took the place of sacrifice, were set up in every Jewish community. 'With the introduction of synagogue worship', says Eavey, 'religion became much more a matter of teaching and learning.'[7] Hengel sees Greek influences intruding at this point, especially in the relative professionalisation of teaching[8] (See next section.)

The Jewish elementary school developed in the synagogue with boys over five learning the three R's, though the primary aim was to teach the Scriptures and encourage the memorisation of large portions of the law. This did not, however, reduce the emphasis on basic religious nurture occurring in the home. A well-taught adult community was the better able to keep up the educative rituals and recitations which were meant to happen at home.

Adults continued to be learners, as the *torah* was expounded week by week in the synagogue. It is worth noting that nobody thought it unusual that on a visit to Nazareth Jesus the layman-carpenter was invited to read aloud a passage from the law and then offer expository comment. Admittedly, they got more than they bargained for! (Luke 4:16–29.)

On the evidence, Barclay's summary seems indisputable:

> In any examination of Jewish education it is essential to remember two things — first, that Jewish education was almost exclusively religious education; and second, that, at all periods of it, the centre is the home, and the responsibility of teaching the child is something that the parent cannot evade, if he is to satisfy the Law of God.[9]

Schools and Sophists in Greek Times

The high culture of ancient Greece has left an indelible mark on the western world. Reinhold Niebuhr identifies it as one of the two main sources of our culture, the other being the Hebraic.[10] In his view, the Hellenistic legacy has attained such dominance that a corrective is now needed. Certainly, despite the many good things we may attribute to this source, the Christian in search of biblical theories of action must often pull against its persuasive values in many areas, including theology, philosophy, morality, and education.

The appropriate case study for our purposes is the Hellenistic view of teaching and schooling. The first thing that strikes us is the rise of the professional teacher, offering his services as tutor to the children of those affluent enough to meet his fees. From as early as the seventh century before Christ such people were a feature of Greek social life. Three kinds of specialist teacher emerged: one concentrating on language and letters; one on music and dance; and the third on gymnastics or physical culture. Often they settled in fixed locations and developed schools to which the children were brought daily by their slave-supervisors (Gk. *paidogōgos*).

Amongst the echelon of these professional teachers were the sophists. By the fifth century BC, higher level studies had developed around wandering scholars who offered young men above the age of fifteen 'instruction for fees . . ., particularly very extensive training in speech, emphasizing grammar, rhetoric and oratory'.[11] Their label derived from *sophistes*, the Greek word for one who practises wisdom. A primary assumption behind their approach was that they were training leaders of society, not workers who had to earn their living. The next basic assumption was that the correct way to prepare such people was to cultivate the mind, enhancing rationality.

The best of the sophists achieved considerable social repute and also developed schools in fixed locations. Socrates, possibly the greatest of them all, encouraged persistent questioning of the unreflective beliefs held by his contemporaries with respect to knowledge, moral values and politics. His striving for honesty and objectivity established the ideal of impartial, critical enquiry which has rightly become a goal in modern scholarship and scientific research.

It has also had much to do with the expectations we now have of professional teachers. They are to be people who are well-versed in their subject matter, capable of introducing their pupils into the high culture of the day in such a way that they achieve a significant level of critical detachment from the unexamined mores and traditions of home and society. Cultivation of the mind confers rational autonomy of action on the individual, and (it is assumed) prompts him to work for the good of all.

So far as intellectual development was concerned, Socrates' approach bore impressive fruit. His pupil Plato, and Aristotle, who in turn was Plato's pupil, exercised their minds with great skill on many subjects in science, philosophy, ethics, and politics. Plato also had much to say about education, and though his views have been criticised at many points by modern theorists, his influence is still to be reckoned with. Many rational humanists are closer to Plato in their basic assumptions about human nature than they are prepared to admit.

This is particularly the case with respect to the Greek confidence in the moral power of right reason. To know what is good is to want it, Socrates maintained. Enlighten the mind and our young men will be motivated to work for the good of the *polis*, or political community, with insight and wisdom. Plato reflected this confidence faithfully in his earlier writings on education, particularly *The Republic*. But there are signs in his later work *The Laws* of a more sceptical awareness that human nature is also subject to a strong pull of self-interest and egotism.

It may be that Plato was coming to terms with the disillusioning experience of seeing how some of his own students behaved when they obtained political power. But the problem had already arisen in the activities of many sophists. Socrates himself severely criticised those sophists who were more concerned to encourage individual cleverness and the ability to manipulate people by one's eloquence, than they were to promote commitment to truth and the common good.[12] What he failed to see was that rationality is not the summative quality of human personhood, though it is an important tool in the achievement of human purposes. Hence, reason by itself will not produce the good person. And a concept of education which makes the development of reason its highest aim will not adequately serve either society or the individual.

We have seen then that the professionalisation of teaching in ancient Greece was a mixed blessing. There were permanent gains in the development of a respect for the power of human reason and a tradition of scholarship to be preserved by the intellectual education of each rising generation.

More questionable was the restriction of such an education to the fee-paying elite, which Plato baptized philosophically by developing a class-structured theory of human nature. This theory still underlies the operation of some exclusive independent schools. Economic limitations prevented the majority of Greeks from benefiting from the schooling then available, whereas in modern technological societies mass education has become economically feasible. The question is, however, can the educational theory of the Greeks be generalised to the masses?

The answer is: probably not. Its emphasis on critical rationality, already under strain when enjoined on the leisured classes, is altogether too limited a goal to animate mass education. In a sense, the majority of people in modern western societies have obtained the gift of leisure, but they not only want to use it for reflective thinking, but for loving and travelling and helping others and earning more money, etc. Most people are also workers, and need to be given an appreciation of the place of work in their lives which both dignifies it and keeps it in perspective. Greek pedagogy cannot help us here.

There is another fundamental area in which Greek models are deficient. They undervalue the family and parental responsibility. Affluent parents employed guardians to mind their children and take them to school. There was minimal social interchange between men and women. Despite Plato's willingness to educate boys and girls together (until the girls' lesser ability streamed them out of the later levels!), he only saw girls as inferior males. His famous dialogue on love passes quickly over heterosexual love, titters about some of the more fleshly forms of homosexual activity, and praises the intellectual love possible between men as the highest kind of love.

The delegation of parental responsibility for nurture to other persons, particularly to professional servants, has always been a tendency in affluent families. One testimony to this is the centuries-old popularity of boarding schools. In the industrial era, however, this tendency has become institutionalised to a remarkable degree in the multiplication of the 'helping professions' such as social workers, welfare officers, legal and medical practitioners, and public servants generally. They have an appropriate bureaucratic model ready to hand: school systems with professional teachers, to which parents commit their children with a comparatively open cheque. A popular response, when some social need or problem is brought to light, is to say 'leave it to the school'. Countries committed to extensive social engineering have no qualms about using the schools to implant their social doctrines and inhibit the influence of the home.

It is neither fanciful nor unfair to attribute such attitudes to our legacy from the Greeks. Indeed the noted philosopher Karl Popper claimed a direct line of descent between Plato and Karl Marx, in his book *The Open Society and Its Enemies.*[13] Even Christians have been persuaded to invest heavily in this delegation of responsibility to the school. We will see why this has happened when we come to the medieval and reformation periods.

Our next touch-down in history will be the pattern of NT Christianity. Kevin Giles considers that the Greek legacy has had a particularly distorting effect on our modern understanding of the teaching style of Jesus and his followers.[14] One might reasonably expect to the contrary that there would have been considerable Greek influence at the time on Jesus and the early church. Despite the decline of Greek political power before the legions of Rome, the Hellenisation of the ancient world at a cultural level had been substantial. Greek was the language of culture and commerce and the common medium in which many Jews read their OT, using the *Septuagint* translation. The fact is, however, that the influence of Greek *values* in the NT was actually minimal! This may be attributed to the robustness of the Judaic tradition in which our Lord was raised.

Teaching in the New Testament

It is hard to detect *any* direct Greek influence on the early church's understanding of the teacher's role. What comes through is soundly Hebraic, and in several crucial ways continuous with the OT. The word 'school', for instance, is as absent from the NT as from the OT, notwithstanding the evolution of Jewish schools and centres of higher learning around this time.[15] The matrices of teaching were the home and the gathered community of believers.

First, Christ and the apostles reaffirm the attitudes of concern for the nurture of children (Mark 9:36–42; Eph 6:4). The point is not laboured, since it is a basic axiom already taken for granted in Jewish circles. Barclay points out that:

> The New Testament lays down no kind of curriculum of training for the child; the New Testament knows nothing about religious education and nothing about schools; for the New Testament is certain that the only training which really matters is given within the home, and that there are no teachers so effective for good or evil as parents are.[16]

Secondly, the gathered congregation of believers is a learning environment, in which all in a general sense are teachers, sharing their insights and experiences of the Christian walk for the edification of all, and seeking to enlighten others about the way of life (Col 3:16; 2 Cor 5:19). Christianity is not a mystery religion; God has allowed his secrets to become public property, and the Good News is for all — 'Go and teach'.

Thirdly, the aim of this proclamation is not merely intellectual enlightenment, nor legalistic conformity of behaviour to Christian norms. It is commitment built on understanding, the kind of understanding which animates conduct and enables us even in complex situations 'to distinguish good from evil' (1 Cor 14:20; Js 1:22–25; Heb 5:12–14). From the initial resolve to follow Christ, we are to have and to develop a clear-headed awareness of what we are doing. It is interesting to see how insistent Jesus was on this. Many were attracted by his words and works. Consistently, his response was to test the depth of their commitment by challenging them to weigh up all the factors and be clear about what it would cost (Matt 8:18–22; 15:21–28; Mark 7:14–23; 10:17–31; Luke 7:36–50; 14:25–33; John 4:1–28; 14:21–30). Indoctrination is sub-Christian.

The teaching ministry of the community of believers had no end; it was not as though some had already attained all they needed to know. There is always more to learn and more to share about the will of God and the way of life. In this, and in all the previous respects, the best of the Judaic heritage flows through into Christianity.

The NT, however, does add something new and distinctive. While it is true that in a general sense all are teachers, there is a sense in which some are gifted with a special ministry of teaching on behalf of the whole body of believers. When a group of believers begins to develop the marks of a caring community, the Spirit of God knits them into the body of Christ. Under these conditions, the grace (*charis*) of Christ becomes evident in the variety of spiritual gifts (*charismata*) which emerge. Each member of the body is necessary to the health of the whole (Rom 12:3–8; 1 Cor 12:1–31; Eph 4:1–16).

Some gifts are enabling gifts of leadership within the whole body, which equip all members to exercise more effectively their individual gifts of ministry in the wider world.[17] One of these enabling gifts is teaching. It is bestowed on certain individuals for the sake of the body, not the member. If a person covets the gift for his own prestige, then not only is he at risk personally, but he is also putting the body at risk. 'We who teach will be judged more strictly.' Already, lamented Paul, there are some who, having aspired to be teachers of the law of God, have led many people astray (1 Tim 1:6–7; cf. Js 3:1).

This special enabling gift of teaching, dependent as it is on the activity of the Holy Spirit, is in continuity with the OT where from time to time inspirited individuals were raised up to recall the covenant people to the law of God. But in the NT the phenomenon is firmly anchored in congregational body-life, and the purpose is to enable *all* members to exercise the gifts generated in them by the continuously present Spirit of God.

Is this then the Christian analogue of the professional teacher in Greek culture? Not at all. Where the latter is a paid professional concerned mainly with the intellectual education of an elite, the charismatic teacher is a voluntary member of a community of faith acknowledged as having been called to guide the spiritual development of all. God is sovereignly free to confer the gift of teaching on someone with secular teacher-training or someone without such training as he wills. It is not surprising if he does capitalise on a person's previous formal training (as it appears he frequently does), but he is not bound by this precondition.

As to the questions of payment and full-time occupation, the Scriptures are flexible. Local needs and circumstances determine this. One who is paid for full-time service by the body at one time, may at another contribute his or her gifts voluntarily while in secular employment. Status as such is not a consideration. There is an interesting case where Paul urges Titus in Crete to curb the activities of those who are teaching, as the Authorised Version bluntly puts it, 'for filthy lucre's sake' (Tit 1:11 AV). The vehemence of this remark implies that Paul saw here an attempt to mimic the careerism of the sophists, and he was having none of it.

Schools and Clerics in the Middle Ages

We have barely moved beyond the NT era before the open and dynamic character of Christian body-life begins to yield to the creeping paralysis of bureaucracy. With hindsight we can regret this, though at the time the options were doubtless not so clear. It is always easier to adopt what appear to be safe human expedients than to face threats to survival with a patient trust in the Spirit of God.

And threats there were, both inside and out. Internally, heresies reared their heads, and it seemed that tougher disciplinary measures were needed. Externally, persecution and ostracism seemed best countered by closing ranks and acting in concert.

Strength and continuity of leadership depended, it appeared, on the professionalisation of leadership roles. As a consequence of this an unbiblical distinction came into being between clergy and laity.

The challenge from outside was intellectual as well as political. Coupled with the fact that Christianity was increasingly attracting members of the educated classes into its ranks, this led to pressures for formal instruction and the development of a scholarly apologetic. Classes for new converts were formalised into catechumenal schools, while the training of clergy led to the creation of catechetical schools.

Origen (c. 185–254), who was head of the catechetical school at Alexandria, is generally credited with the first significant attempt to bring the Christian apologetic into the mainstream of Graeco-Roman culture, making it an intellectual force to be reckoned with. He also insisted that Greek culture was necessary to the training of Christian leaders.[18] This did much to hasten the professionalisation of both the clergy and the function of teaching. Eavey notes that the later episcopal and cathedral schools which evolved under the oversight of the bishops and church councils

> . . . intensified the tendency begun in the catechetical schools to take less and less interest in the instruction of all Christians and to form a special priestly class. In time, the result was an intellectual aristocracy in the church, with much ignorance among the masses.[19]

The schools we have mentioned so far, however, were initially schools for instruction in the Christian faith. But what of general education? The answer is likely to be surprising to those who assume that the present commitment of most churches to church-based schools merely reflects the consistent policies of earliest Christianity.

First, it should be remembered that schools were a familiar social institution in NT times and the centuries immediately following. The Greeks had them, and wealthy Romans followed suit. Moreover it became a matter of government policy to establish Roman schools wherever the empire spread its bounds.

Boyd claims that by the end of the second century, Roman schools were practically universal in distribution[20] though they remained the preserve of the well-to-do. In them, the best of the Greek and Roman literatures was studied, set within the world-view of paganism.

What were the Christians to do? The apparently obvious answer was to set up their own schools. But for various reasons they did not do this. Ancient historian Edwin Judge points out that the early Christians instructed their children in religious matters at home and in the congregation, not in schools. Those who were more affluent and wanted their children to receive a cultural broadening sent them to the pagan schools, and it was from such a background that the faith obtained many of its greatest apologists in later years. The church itself did not get into the business of general education until the fourth century.[21] The Christians of that time obviously believed in the power of nurture in the home and the church to counteract the pagan influences in the Roman curriculum.

Nevertheless, it was a risky path to take, in the same sense that it is risky to live according to Christ's expectation that we will witness *in* the world while not being *of* it (John 17:14–18). We need to come to an understanding of the world and the way it thinks in order to communicate our faith to it. But we have to guard against acceptance of its values and submission to its way of thinking.

There were individual examples of Christian catechetical schools broadening their curriculum to include the tasks of general education — Origen's school at Alexandria was one — but the church did not become generally involved until the emperor Constantine embraced Christianity as the state religion. Now the ethos of the Roman schools was under siege. For a brief moment it seemed that Julian in 362AD would be able to turn the clock back when he decreed that Christians were forbidden to teach in the schools of the empire.[22] But his death the following year left the door open to Christian influences.

Thereafter the public schools for grammar and rhetoric were in decline, while the trend accelerated in Christian schools in cathedrals and elsewhere to add the functions of general education (though still for a minority) to their curriculum. A new factor which hastened these processes was the invasion of Europe by successive waves of barbarians in the fifth century. As the political unity and civil control of the empire collapsed, the church came further into the field of general education. It was motivated, if Judge is correct, more by a desire to save a useful social institution from collapse, than a need to preserve the faith of the faithful.

The barbarian invasion had another fateful effect on the trend towards professionalised schooling and teaching. In many cases, higher learning survived only in the monasteries, hidden in libraries where literary works were laboriously copied to ensure preservation, but were rarely studied in a critical spirit. These establishments owed their formation to Hellenistic ideas, especially the teachings of the Neoplatonists. As developed by Plotinus in the third century, Neoplatonism taught the inferiority of the material world in contrast to the world of the spirit. Eventually it led many devout Christians to believe that the path to holiness and a higher plane of spirituality was to place themselves under the self-denying lifestyle of the cloistered monk or nun. This further accentuated the gulf between cleric and layman.

At the high point of the Middle Ages, when culture was flowering in the twelfth and thirteenth centuries, an impressive amalgam of Christian and Graeco-Roman values held the social fabric together. The various gifts of the Holy Spirit had been domesticated and assigned to the clergy. Even the qualification for admission to higher studies in general was ordination for life. The linguistic connection between the term 'cleric', meaning an ordained man, and what in business practice we now often term 'clerical duties' is no accident, for the clergy became the secretaries and bureaucrats of the western world; a class of people trained in the literary-academic mode, situated between the aristocracy trained in chivalry on the one hand and the peasantry trained for their crafts by home and craft guild on the other.[23]

It was a far cry from the democratic spirit of community in the Judaic and NT traditions. Lay people were a lower order of believer, assumed to possess no gifts relevant to the building up of the community of believers. (If they had shown any, would we not have schooled them and ordained them?) The clergy were the ones chosen to exercise the gifts, and access to the gifts was through the professionalised route of schooling, based on a curriculum heavily indebted to Greek views of man and society, especially as regards the saving power of natural reason.

And what of the nurture of children? The trends I have been describing reduced the spiritual standing of parents and encouraged the attitude of 'leave it to the church'. At the same time, however, church dignitaries in formally Christian societies were tending to take for granted the status of their parishioners as Christians, provided that they had undergone that ceremony of identification with the visible church called baptism. The doctrine of baptismal regeneration removed the sense of obligation to enlarge the child's or the church member's *understanding* of his faith relationship with God, for wasn't his eternal future already secure? But lest he falter in the works of faith, such as giving tithes to the church and alms to the poor, there were the sanctions of penance, purgatory and excommunication which church authorities were empowered to invoke.

Some children, however, *were* considered for Christian education. They were the ones who qualified for training as choristers or priests. It was they who formed the base of the cathedral and choir schools and, if they were of sufficient ability, went on to the universities which developed from the twelfth century onwards out of the more illustrious schools in places like Paris, Bologna and Oxford. It is probable that more students of ability (regardless of their means) had access to university education in this period than at any subsequent time up to the growth period after the Second World War.[24]

But whereas in the present day the rest have universal access at least to primary and secondary school, in the medieval period they remained unenlightened and in fear and fealty of mother church. The processes of education, both Christian and liberal, were animated by the Hellenistic model of education for leadership rather than the Hebraic model of the enlightenment and gifts-development of all.

Footnotes

1. Except where otherwise indicated all biblical quotations are from the *New International Version* (London: Hodder and Stoughton, 1979).
2. W. Barclay, *Educational Ideals in the Ancient World* (Grand Rapids: Baker 1974) 19–22.
3. The Hebrew word *torah* originally meant 'instruction'. It was the use of the Greek *nomos* in translation which brought the word 'law' through into English translation. I am indebted to Dr. John Olley for this observation.
4. And women. See, for example, 2 Sam 14:2.
5. Thus M. Hengel, *Judaism and Hellenism* (tr. John Bowden, Philadelphia: Fortress, 1981) 79.
6. C.B. Eavey, *History of Christian Education* (Chicago: Moody, 1964) 63.
7. *Ibid.*, 64. See also Hengel, *Hellenism*, 79.
8. Hengel, *Hellenism*, 81f.
9. Barclay, *Ideals*, 17. For reasons that will appear later, I regret his use of the word 'education', which is not a biblical word.
10. Reinhold Niebuhr, 'The Two Sources of Western Culture' in *The Christian Idea of Education* (ed. Edmund Fuller; New Haven: Yale University, 1957) 237–54.
11. R.L. Pounds, *The Development of Education in Western Culture* (New York: Appleton-Century-Crofts, 1968) 47.
12. Hence the modern meaning of the word 'sophistry': reasoning which seems plausible but is chiefly a device to manipulate the hearer.
13. K.R. Popper, *The Open Society and Its Enemies* (London: Routledge & Kegan Paul, 1945).
14. K.N. Giles, 'Teachers and Teaching in the Church: Part I,' *JCE* 70 (1981) 5–6.
15. The one use of *scholē* in Acts 19:9 has no normative significance. Paul simply used the premises of Tyrannus as an *ad hoc* teaching venue. Where the Authorised Version refers to a schoolmaster in Gal 3:24, we find that the reference is not to a teacher but to the *paidogōgos* or guardian mentioned earlier.
16. Barclay, *Ideals*, 236.
17. H.R. Snyder (*The Community of the King* [Downers Grove: IVP, 1978] 76–94) has a balanced analysis of these concepts and distinctions.
18. Eavey, *History*, 89.
19. *Ibid.*, 90.
20. William Boyd and Edmund J. King, *The History of Western Education* (London: Adam and Charles Black, 1972) 75.
21. E.A. Judge, 'The Conflict of Educational Aims in New Testament Thought', *JCE* 9 (1966) 32–45.
22. Boyd and King, *Western Education*, 87.
23. T.L. Jarman, *Landmarks in the History of Education* (London: John Murray, 1970) 55.
24. This observation was suggested by a remark of H. Rashdall's in the *Cambridge Mediaeval History* (Cambridge: Cambridge University, 1929) 6:559–600.

3

The Rise of Schooled Societies

There is a crucial difference between societies in which the school is seen as one amongst several different kinds of educational provision, and those in which the school is viewed as the central and most universal way of making this provision. Describing the situation in England, Wardle points out that 'until the late eighteenth century formal, organized instruction of any kind was confined to a minority.'[1] Before that time, most people received no instruction beyond the home, except that which they picked up in the early months of settling in to a job or learning a trade. At higher social levels, whether for apprenticeship or professional preparation, parents often placed their children in other people's homes or employed tutors to provide instruction in the home.

England came very late to the idea of universal schooling. One of the arguments used by its advocates in the nineteenth century was the fact that several European countries already had state educational systems with compulsory school attendance, notably those countries most affected by the Protestant Reformation. Another factor which helped to swing a reluctant parliament behind the idea was the growing demand for a literate workforce to serve the industrial complex developing in Britain. These two lines of influence need to be understood if we are to comprehend the workings of our present 'schooled' society and to resist illegitimate extensions of this model into church life.

Schools and Teachers in the Reformation

Historians of educational ideas have a tendency to skip over the Reformation educators, though willing enough to salute leaders of the Renaissance such as Erasmus. It seems that they are more comfortable in their quest for relevant educational models with a revival of secular learning looking back to the Greeks than with a revival of religious understanding looking back to the Bible. One historian fairer than most, William Boyd, has been more discerning. He sees the Reformation as ushering in a new phase in education of 'momentous consequences for the future of the world'.[2] In its commitment to the democratic right of all citizens to receive an education suited to their capacities, the Reformation educational model was Hebraic. In its belief that the appropriate vehicle was the school, it was Hellenistic.

The clerical monopoly of the teaching office had been gradually loosening since the fifteenth century,[3] but great numbers of cathedral and grammar schools were still staffed by Catholic clergy when the Reformation broke out. In the resulting confusion, new educational policies were called for, and Martin Luther entered into extensive correspondence with church and municipal authorities to stabilise and extend the provision of schools. He set out a number of principles to which modern educators are more indebted than they usually realise or admit.

First, Luther called for free, compulsory education, available not only to boys but also to girls (whom the Renaissance had largely ignored). This could only be realised if the state took responsibility for guaranteeing the provision of schools. Cities were urged to found and staff them. The curriculum was to be both Christian and liberal including, at secondary level, studies in the classics of Greece and Rome.[4]

A point often overlooked is that Luther did not see this as replacing nurture in the home or learning by other means. 'My idea,' he said, 'is to let boys go to such a school for one or two hours a day, and spend the remainder of the time working at home, learning a trade or doing whatever their parents desired.'[5] In the same passage, he ran contrary to popular attitudes regarding the status of women by pleading that 'in like manner, a girl can surely find time enough to go to school for one hour a day and still attend to all her duties at home.'

The day of universal schooling in Germany had not yet arrived. Religious wars held back the realisation of Luther's vision, but the seed had been sown and encouragement had been given to philanthropic bodies to do their bit towards providing for the education of the masses. By the end of the eighteenth century, Prussia was leading the way with a national system of public schools for all children. It was a significant commentary on Luther's approach that the passage of time had so weakened its religious rationale that a law in 1803 released the schools from the obligation to uphold any particular religious confession.[6] In a pluralistic world, alliance with the state has its dangers.

In Geneva, John Calvin shared the same religious democratic vision as Luther, but differed on the question of *who* should provide schools. He believed that it was desirable to keep the church free of compromising alliances with the secular government. But he also regarded general education as the province of the church, deeming it necessary to ensure that all studies had a theocentric unity.[7] It was his expectation that the state would stand behind this arrangement and protect the church's educational authority. Walker sees this as a carry-over of 'the mediaeval theory of the relations of church and state',[8] and it carried the day in many European countries — for the time being. Boyd indicates the extent of Calvin's influence in the remark that:

> The Huguenots in France, the Reformed Church in Holland, the Puritans in England, the Presbyterians in Scotland, all followed in different ways and with varying success the school and university system of the little Swiss city, and through them Calvinism became as mighty a force in education as in religion.[9]

The most thorough implementation was in Scotland, where John Knox set out to ensure that every church would appoint a schoolmaster to provide rudimentary education for all, every town develop a grammar school, and every large town create a high school or college. Lack of money should not prevent the ablest from going on to university and, indeed, Knox charged the church with the duty of keeping the most able at their studies. As it turned out, though neither church nor parliament accepted the whole of Knox's proposals, Scotland became a country where learning was much sought after, and the schoolmaster or dominie became a highly respected figure. Moreover a working model had been set forth, based on universal, age-graded instruction provided by a pyramidic network of formal educational institutions.

The legacy of the Reformation was therefore ambiguous. It proclaimed the equality of all men and women before God, and their right to an education suited to their status as participating citizens and to their various capacities. But it insisted on the inseparability of general education from teaching for faith-commitment, it foreshadowed the monopolisation of learning by the institution of formal schooling, and it retained the medieval view of the teacher as a religious professional.

These ambiguities can be seen to run together in Calvin's view of the office of teacher. His 1541 Ordinances identified four offices instituted by Christ: pastors, teachers, elders, and deacons. Teachers were those responsible for operating his school system, which combined the tasks of religious training and liberal education.[10] As such they were paid professionals in the church whose role was validated theologically by the teaching on spiritual gifts.

It would be unfair not to acknowledge in passing the educational contributions of the Counter-Reformation, even though this was a Roman Catholic response to the initial stimulus of the Protestant reforms and in several respects derivative. Ignatius Loyola pioneered the establishment of teaching orders in the Roman Catholic Church when he founded the Society of Jesus, which received papal approval in 1540.[11] More democratic and philanthropic in intent than the Jesuits were the Christian Brothers brought together by De La Salle in France in 1682. And there were others. In relation to our argument, however, these worthy endeavours serve merely to reinforce the general thesis that concepts of teaching and schooling continued to be more medieval than scriptural.

Schools for the Industrial Society

In England, the forward-looking ideas of the Puritans[12] were largely driven underground by the restoration of the monarchy and the opposition of the Anglican establishment. The nation therefore entered the nineteenth century lagging behind other European countries in the provision of education for the masses. Where religious arguments had failed, earthier motivations now began to prevail.

England was the first country to experience industrial revolution. Within a few decades, long-established systems of home industry and craft guilds were made obsolescent by machines and factories. Hundreds of people for whom illiteracy had previously been no handicap found themselves in labour pools already swelling with labourers thrown off the farms of England because of agricultural invention and enclosure. In the scramble for survival, young children were sent out to find work to supplement meagre family earnings.

Some consciences were stirred by the impassioned speeches of Christian and socialist reformers, others were more affected by the increasing burden on local councils of providing poor relief. Elementary education was seen to be one of the best remedies for poverty and unemployment, if only because 'inculcating children with the virtues of industry, thrift, and responsibility, which their parents were presumed to lack . . . seemed likely to act as a preventive'.[13]

What finally tipped the scales and brought the parliamentarians and industrialists over to the side of the reformers was the development of industrial processes which required a workforce minimally competent in the three R's and capable of understanding urban society. It was also believed that education in the fourth R — religion — would fix in the labouring heart a proper sense of morality and a respect for the established authorities in society. But there was a limit. The lower classes should not be given too much education. As Wardle summarises:

> Most moderate and liberal opinion favoured elementary education for the labouring classes, provided thet [sic] it was strictly

> limited in content, strongly disciplinary in tone, and was not employed as an instrument for social levelling.[14]

The *compulsory* clause was brought into operation in England in the 1870's, partly as a result of a growing concern for the welfare of children who would otherwise be exploited by their parents. Crime and disease amongst children were horrifying, despite their release from some of the appalling conditions they had experienced in mines and factories before the passing of laws against child labour.

But the other great consideration leading to the legislation of compulsory attendance at school was national development. The architect of the 1870 Education Act, W.E. Forster, stressed the need for England to retain her industrial lead in the face of accelerating competition from other industrialising countries. 'Upon the speedy provision of elementary education,' he said, 'depends our industrial prosperity'.[15]

This is an argument open to continuous extrapolation as the needs of industry become more complex. By the turn of the twentieth century, it was being used in some countries to justify the entry of governments into the provision of *secondary* education and the extension of the school leaving age. After the Second World War it was used to justify the democratisation of *university* entry through the creation of more universities and the provision of financial assistance for poor but worthy matriculants.

In the process, there have been significant changes in the way the community views education. They affect the content of the curriculum, the role of the teacher and the decision about who will provide general education.

With regard to the *curriculum*, there has been a mushrooming of scientific and technological studies. Luther's one or two hours a day might have been enough to cover the four R's, and a liberal education along the lines of the classical curriculum might have sufficed to enable clergy to teach all comers at secondary level, prior to the scientific and industrial revolutions. But we are now in an age where the range of studies relevant to a minimal understanding of, and survival in, one's own society is vast, causing endless debates about what to include, and increasing the degree of specialisation in the teaching profession.

Furthermore, greater specialisation in individual subject areas has reduced the possibility of finding unifying themes and values to hold the curriculum together. Religion, for example, is no longer the recognised source of our basic axioms in studying mathematics or science. And religious studies themselves, where they have not been relegated to the too-hard basket, have become more objective and descriptive. Sheer volume has reduced the proportion of time and attention which can be given to matters of personal faith and relationships within the compulsory curriculum. This may be just as well, for they sit uneasily in such a context anyway, and need attention in alternative and freer learning environments, as I shall argue later.

Secondly, the *role of the teacher* has become more technical and limited. In the framework of compulsory instruction, the teacher is expected to be more objective and impartial, helping the students to grasp and examine for themselves large bodies of data. An impressive body of research has grown up around the act of teaching, increasing the trained teacher's insight and effectiveness. It is no longer sufficient to ask a liberally educated 'gentleman' or 'gentlewoman' to set up a school or teach in a classroom without further preparation. Even the few who are 'born teachers' need professional training to understand the social and psychological factors which constrain their activities in the day school.

But this kind of professionalisation differs in character from the earlier professionalisation of teaching in the medieval period. Then, the teacher was first and foremost a servant of the church, teaching a stable curriculum dominated by religious purposes. Now, the teacher is a servant of the ideal of general education, a process intended to enable individuals to cope with their complex environment and to make intelligent choices about their own commitments. I will examine this further in the next chapter. Teachers still have a kind of moral authority, but it is an authority which comes from knowing their subject, rather than from representing a religious establishment. Where the one person tries to combine both rationales in the one role — as, for example, when a clergyman teaches general subjects — then the stage is set for an often bruising conflict in role-expectations.

Thirdly, the question of *who will control* the provision of general education has become problematic. Since the medieval period, Christians have tended to believe that the church should have a monopoly. Since the industrial revolution, however, the church's supremacy in cultural terms has been diminishing even more rapidly than its numerical base in the population. The sheer logistics of population growth have swung the balance of control over to government. Similarly, the logistics of the knowledge explosion have secularised curriculum content. It is time to ask whether the church needs to maintain a total duplicate provision of general education in order to fulfil its primary mandate to teach the gospel. The effort involved is enormous. And again, I suggest, it is possible that by causing the proclamation of the free gospel of Christ to put on the vestments of compulsory schooling, we impede its effect.

The Sunday School Movement

The church's problematic relationship to general education on the one hand, and the teaching of the faith in its own community of belief on the other, is well illustrated by the history of the Sunday school idea. Like universal schooling, this is now such an accepted feature in Protestant church life that we easily forget that the pattern is not much more than two hundred years old.

The idea first developed in England as a direct outgrowth of the aroused consciences of people touched by the Evangelical Revival of the late eighteenth century.[16] Robert Raikes describes how he was shocked by the behaviour of ragged children in the suburbs of Gloucester on the one day of the week when they were released from employment. He conceived the idea of persuading local school dames to take classes on Sunday catering for such children, and instructing them 'in reading and in the Church catechism'.[17]

Raikes was not the first to think of this, but he spearheaded the movement after 1781, and expansion was explosive. Like many charities of that era, many of the societies promoting

Sunday schools were lay-sponsored and interdenominational. But the trend was to absorb them into denominational structures. As to their coverage, Laqueur estimates that 'very few working-class children after 1830 could have escaped at least a few years in Sunday School'.[18]

There were those who opposed the idea. Politically, some feared that the Sunday schools would breed dissidents and opponents of the established order — an objection also levelled at state involvement in the compulsory schooling which came later. Ecclesiastically, there was unease amongst many clergy at the high level of lay involvement, which threatened their standing as the church's teachers and leaders.[19] Biblically, there were those who feared a tendency amongst parents to off-load their primary responsibility for the spiritual nurture of their children onto these institutions. In retrospect, each of these objections was well-founded.

A further kind of objection came from those who thought it an improper use of the sabbath to teach such secular subjects as reading, writing, arithmetic, and often some manual skills as well, on Sunday.[20] But the general consensus was that neither this nor the previous objections outweighed the value of such schools, and they flourished as one valuable avenue of elementary education. That is, they were not initially meant to be used primarily for religious instruction.

As the nineteenth century progressed, however, child labour was reduced and government day schools began to overtake the original purposes of the Sunday schools. Gradually, denominations turned them towards the purposes of nurture within the faith community, and thus the model of formal schooling was drawn into the service of the gathered church.

The story of the Sunday school in America reveals some important variations from the English story. The main reason for this was the battle in the eighteenth century to declare the growing number of government schools 'secular' in the sense that they should exhibit no bias towards any religious sect. The struggle was resolved in a radical way by excluding *all* religious instruction from the public school curriculum. This provoked the churches to look for alternative ways of attending to their children's religious and moral instruction. Some, of course, found in this state of affairs an additional reason to withdraw to private schools. Others saw in Raikes' work in England a model to follow.

At first some of the early Sunday schools included the philanthropic objectives of elementary education for the needy which had been the primary motivation for the efforts of Raikes and other reformers. But the faith-nurture objective soon became uppermost, and dominated the charter of the American Sunday School Union which was formed in 1824.[21] This body was very active at an interdenominational level in promoting teacher-training and issuing printed resources, including a five-year cycle of uniform Bible readings on which to base weekly instruction.

Eavey notes that in this period four different avenues of religious instruction were tried, out of which one emerged as by far the most preferred solution. The four were: the public school, the home, the church day school, and the Sunday school.[22] It was on the last of these that most Christians pinned their hopes.

The movement grew steadily, with Sunday schools being gradually drawn into denominational frameworks. State, national and, from 1875, international conventions fostered the exchange of ideas and a trend developed towards acceptance of the educational principles which were being worked out in the world of secular education.

Brubacher sees something of a crisis developing at the beginning of the twentieth century. He describes it as a conflict between two theories of moral education: the Sunday school approach stressing the prior need for personal conversion, the public school approach relying on enlightenment through education. As Brubacher tells the story, the crisis was resolved by the formation of the Religious Education Association in 1903, which pressed for a new emphasis in Sunday schools on education rather than evangelism.[23] Eavey reads the situation differently, seeing the R.E.A. as a platform for the liberal theology of the time, which provoked evangelical churches to come together under a different banner in 1910.[24]

There was a general decline in the Sunday school movement in the period between the first two World Wars. It is doubtful whether all the reasons for this are yet understood. Since the Second World War, however, there has been a resurgence of enthusiasm and development, under the more comprehensive label of 'Christian Education'. Though there is evidence of some interesting tendencies to look to learning environments other than the 'schooling model' — some associated with the name of John Westerhoff III — it is fair to say that the keystone of most programmes is still the Sunday school, frequently operating in grades for all ages including adults. The schooled mentality is well-entrenched.

In summary, a pattern originally pioneered by churches for the purpose of providing some kind of general education for the needy has mutated into the main preferred strategy for building up the informed commitment of the children of Christians. Eavey's criticism of theologically liberal educators as being too enamoured with the ideals of Greek culture[25] possibly may not bite deep enough. Perhaps his own attachment to the Sunday school idea itself is open to the same criticism.

The Deschooling Critique

At this point we need to be aware of a mounting body of criticism of the school idea, coming from several different quarters. I will simplify a diffuse range of literature by speaking of two general lines of argument: the libertarian and the marxist.

The libertarian[26] critique is well represented by Ivan Illich's best-seller *Deschooling Society*. Illich's views were developed in the course of working in Puerto Rico to relieve poverty. Initially, he says, he 'never questioned the value of extending obligatory schooling to all people'.[27] But he came to believe that schools are a means of domesticating the poor to keep them in their place, quenching initiative and turning out obedient consumers who keep the wheels of a growth economy turning. 'In a schooled world,' he says, 'the road to happiness is paved with a consumer's index', and, in another sparkling aphorism: 'People who have been schooled down to size let unmeasured experience slip out of their hands'.[28]

This could simply be brilliant, over-simplified rhetoric. And some of it is. But Illich makes a number of valid points which cannot be thus lightly dismissed, particularly about the concepts of school and teacher. Analysing the first, he defines school as 'the age-specific, teacher-related process requiring full-time attendance at an obligatory curriculum'.[29] Upon this institution, society is putting an increasing range of responsibilities, encouraged, perhaps, by the past history of schooling in which the church combined the tasks of general education and faith-nurture. The modern school then is not only expected to take all learning under its wing, but also the functions of welfare and attitude formation which have been either neglected or badly done in the home. If society has a problem, 'leave it to the school'.

But the school, says Illich, is intrinsically anti-educational. It discourages informal learning, curiosity and self-reliance. It packages its wares in compulsory curriculum and graded certificates of achievement, so that having the necessary piece of paper becomes more important than having the skills it is supposed to represent. We may add that it invades the privacy and freedom of the learner by insisting that he reveal himself in response to compulsory testing and instructions to write personal journals. It labels children on the basis of their position on the normal curve of statistical distribution, depriving them of uniqueness and self-esteem.

As I. Lister points out, "a result of the mass system of compulsory schooling in many 'advanced' countries is a confrontation between teachers and pupils".[30] The high school is frequently an environment of alienation, not because the teachers are deliberately wounding their students — many try to be compassionate and caring — but because the very structure within which teachers and learners have been thrown together intrinsically inhibits constructive voluntary relationships. Characteristics such as formal learning fragmented by the period bell, tests and grades, mass teaching and compulsory subjects, work against such countervailing influences as individualised attention and counselling, more informal methods of teaching, and freer interpersonal relationships.

This critique is as applicable to the Christian school as the state school, for it is dealing with the hidden curriculum of the schooling model itself, not with the beliefs and values promoted by the official curriculum.

How ought we to treat such criticisms? Illich's apocalyptic vision calls for a deschooled society in which learning environments are of a much freer and voluntary kind. It is an over-optimistic scenario, in which the rich and talented are likely to get richer while the poor become more disadvantaged, despite what Illich says. Many writers, while acknowledging that Illich has put his finger on a number of weak spots in the schooling model, accuse him of ignoring the credit side of the ledger. In particular, they point to the general raising of community awareness, the more articulate representation of sectional needs and interests, and the more effective deployment of the workforce. It is also worth noting that all the most articulate critics of schooling are themselves products of this form of education.

It would seem that a balanced response to appraisals of the institution of schooling requires an acknowledgment of both its strengths and its limitations. Schools *do* perform a valuable service in introducing children to the wider cultural environment and providing some survival skills, both of a cognitive and a social kind. They *can* serve as a very effective window on the world (though not the only one). And they can free children from some of the prejudices and narrow perspectives which restricted home environments may have given them. Such gains are important both to self development and to the ability to tolerate one's neighbours in a pluralistic community.

But the schooling model is less effective in arousing a desire for the good, a respect for persons, and a sense of purpose in life. Partly, this is because we are still too locked in to the literary-academic style of the Greek tradition, whereas children display a wide range of other abilities as well. Some do better in artistic-creative areas, others in manual constructive; some have special potential to lead groups, others to enrich the sphere of interpersonal relationships. Schools (and Sunday schools) tend to be too narrow in their focus on a certain range of intellectual skills.

Even if such defects were remedied, however, there would remain the need to complement what schools do with learning and counselling opportunities in freer environments. One way is to give more attention to voluntary extra-curricular activities within the school itself. Another is to attach a much higher priority to voluntary groups beyond the school, and to the provision of resources for informal learning along some of the lines suggested by Illich. Experiments of this kind are already occurring in many places, through public libraries, community education centres and activity groups. Thoughtful studies are multiplying of what one book refers to as 'alternatives in education'[31], and we may reasonably hope that the over-popularity of the schooling model will begin to be counter-balanced by other models.

Compulsion, Learning and Commitment

Such moves will be merely band-aid strategies, however, unless we come to terms with underlying questions about the nature of persons and their reactions to compulsion. I have dealt at more length with this issue elsewhere,[32] but a few comments will suffice to indicate its importance to the Christian teacher, whether in church or secular contexts.

Christians believe that human beings have a genuine power of choice. Though they may be constricted by inherited characteristics such as a violent temper, or by environmental pressures such as, in an extreme case, the conquest of one's society by an occupying army, there always remains some scope for personal decision. Without it we would be no more than animals or robots.

There *are* human beings who try to treat other human beings as animals or robots, and to rule them either by conditioning or coercion. But total success always eludes them because of the human being's capacity to think and choose. At worst the captor can enforce outward obedience to his orders, but he can never be sure that the defiant spirit does not still flicker behind those veiled eyes, waiting its chance to be free of his over-ruling.

The illustration is not fanciful for an essay on schooling, because more than one researcher has noted the number of features which schools and prisons have in common. Thus Arnstine points out that both have compulsory attendance, both control movements in space and time (by 'cells and bells!'), both lengthen the time to be served if the subject misbehaves ('detention' or 'staying in'), and both reward good behaviour by early release ('getting out early').[33]

What we have before us in the classroom are not just organisms reacting to stimulation, nor even just learners, but centres of personal consciousness capable to some extent (which we can expand) of self-determination. When we seek to teach them 'facts', or separate items of information, they do not feel threatened by the game we are inviting them to play (unless of course we push them too fast and then hold them up to comparison with quicker learners). So they do what they are asked, at varying levels of seriousness.

However, when we move on to teach concepts and ways of viewing the world as in, say, history or science, they sense that we are trying to shape their actual minds, the way they think. It is now more likely that we will meet with resistance (unless we explain our intentions and motives very patiently) because in these areas we are getting closer to the self-image each person is developing.

If we then take the further step of trying to influence attitudes and change values, then the resistance increases even more dramatically. 'Who is this person,' the self says, 'who is trying to change me when I can't get away? His demands for information about how I feel and what I believe invade my privacy. I have no right of appeal; I am in the school's custody. Even if what he is attempting to teach is good and valuable, my first impulse is to resist, to pretend if necessary, and keep my soul intact.'

Under these conditions, teachers ought to be far more ethical and respectful about the way in which they wield their given authority to compel learning in the classroom. They may by all means attempt to enlighten, inform and sensitise their charges, but any attempt to make them adopt certain values for living, or to test them for holding certain moral or religious beliefs, will violate the teacher-pupil relationship.

Something very significant happens, however, when the teacher meets the learner in a voluntary context. The rules of the game change greatly, especially if the teacher is a voluntary worker not being paid for his services (as in the leadership of say a church youth group). The learner attends such a group of his own free will, and can withdraw if he feels pressured. The leaders have no other disciplinary sanction than to exclude uncooperative persons from the group, a move that is likely to be self-defeating if the group's aim is outreach.

To compensate for this loss of *power*, there is a gain in potential *influence*. The leader must appeal to reason, get to know the individual's interests, and relate to him on a more equal and friendly footing. But it is also possible and permissible in such an environment to commend certain beliefs and values more effectively. The learner hears a leader trying to persuade where he cannot enforce; he sees that leader's commitment being lived out in the way he relates to others informally in the group; possibly the sincerity of the leader's profession is reinforced if it is known he is not on the organisation's payroll. He is commending his faith for love, not money.

The learner finds himself in the position of being able to 'try on' the value-stance commended to him, in the group, without having to fear formal assessment at the end. There is evidence that the voluntary group has great potential to change attitudes, to command a hearing for unfashionable points of view, and to recruit willing disciples. That is after all the story of the church in its best moments. Its worst moments have been when it tried to evangelise by force, whether psychological or physical.

There are therefore good reasons for Christians to adopt a critical stance towards some of the central assumptions of the schooled society, and analogous structures within the church. Schooling is a tool good for some purposes, but too clumsy for others. We have put too many of our eggs in this basket to the neglect of alternative settings for learning, including the home and the voluntary group.

Schools and Social Control

A different kind of critique of the schooled society is coming from marxist sources. In contrast to Illich's analysis, the marxist analysis presupposes that human beings are entirely creatures of the existing social order, conditioned to think a certain way by the influences bearing in upon them after birth from the home and the particular social class to which they belong.

Recent marxist critics of the western school argue that it has operated as a tool in the hands of the ruling elite — often described in America as the 'military-industrial establishment' — to condition the populace to the capitalist way of running society. By cultivating a consumer mentality, it is argued, the elite have kept the minds of the masses on material comforts and dulled their awareness of the contradictions of wealth and poverty, power and powerlessness in their society. By standardising curriculum and test batteries, those servants of the elite, the teachers, have 'domesticated the labour force'[34] and helped to predetermine job suitability.

But it is also part of the marxist analysis to say that much of this has occurred without deliberate forethought; market forces caused it to fall out this way, and the planners were led to create the structures they did by the class interests which determined their modes of thought. Hence schools are largely middle-class institutions favouring the advantaged and discriminating against working class children and ethnic minorities.

There is enough truth in this analysis to hurt. On a smaller scale, many of the moves to set up Christian schools in recent years in the USA have been intended more to enhance the economic life-chances of the children of white middle-class Christians and to circumvent legislation requiring public school systems to integrate black and white children, than to promote the message of Jesus Christ. Again, Australian analysts have noted how, in general, inner city schools tend to get less financial consideration than those in the more affluent suburbs, because their resident communities have less access to the political power-brokers.

But if we are always captives of our class consciousness how can things ever be any different? The marxist answer is that those who reject their class's interests by identifying with the revolutionary struggle for human equality become co-operators in a historical process that will eventually see the dawn of a classless society in which human freedom will at last become a possibility. The classical marxist regards this claim as unarguable because it derives from a 'scientific' analysis of social change. Developing a critical consciousness about one's former entrapment in the mind-set of the oppressor class does not, however, extend to keeping an open, critical mind about the rightness of communist strategies designed to overthrow capitalist economies. The non-marxist must view such dogmatism as an act of faith, not a scientifically verified theory, and one which is the more dangerous for its claim to be beyond criticism.

The outcome of all this for a theory of schooling is that the modern marxist does not reject schooling but argues for its use to achieve revolutionary objectives. In the marxist state, schools become an acknowledged tool of the official ideology, shaping the consciousness of the young in the image of the collective socialist society. In a capitalist or under-developed country, the strategy must be to undermine the stability of that country's political-economic system by creating a climate of dissidence and liberation movements in the schools.[35]

It is hard to argue with people who hold such views especially when however rational one's arguments may appear to be, they have decided beforehand that nothing you can say will be valid because it merely rationalises your own class interests. It is also discouraging to find Christians who embrace a similar view of the function of the school to that of marxists, and propose to indoctrinate as many pupils as possible into the belief that their particular brand of Christianity is beyond criticism. By taking this line, they concede the deterministic view of human nature held by marxists and deprive their pupils of the right to make their own informed choice for or against Christ.

In any case, to all but marxists there must be some significance in the evidence that even our present fallible school systems appear to have an enlightening effect on the general populace.

This 'apparently inescapable liberalizing effect of education,' as Wardle calls it,[36] has often confounded those who sponsored school systems with more limited objectives in mind. Even when school policy makers saw their role as defenders of the status quo, says Wardle,

> One of the principal results of their efforts was to raise their pupils' levels of aspiration, while they conspicuously failed to prevent them from questioning the social and political establishment.[37]

This comment returns us to a previous observation that the educational strategy of schooling is best adapted to enlightening students about the world, their culture and its options, increasing their capacity both for understanding and empathy. We should welcome rather than be dismayed by its pluralism, provided that it deals fairly with the options it presents, giving due representation to the Christian world view while inviting rational analysis of that view and allowing encounter with other alternative views abroad in our community.

But since we have said that a complete theory of education will also concern itself with teaching strategies and learning environments other than those provided by the school, we will insist on the complementary role of such other agencies as the home, churches and voluntary groups, especially in matters of evangelism and value formation.

In modern industrial society, formal education and voluntary communities of commitment need each other. The school sharpens the powers of thinking and feeling and enlarges cultural understanding. It is ethically obliged, however, to stop short of trying to persuade students to commit themselves to a particular belief system. The voluntary group provides a community of commitment in which the individual may pursue his explorations to the point of identification with that group and its ideals. But without schooling he would be much less well equipped to weigh up the merits of the value-stance represented by the group, and to make a responsible and informed personal choice. This conclusion is not dissimilar to the one the early Christians came to, when wondering what to do about the schools of their time.

Footnotes

1. D. Wardle, *The Rise of the Schooled Society* (London: Routledge and Kegan Paul, 1974) 1.
2. Boyd and King, *Western Education*, 183.
3. *Ibid.*, 157.
4. Martin Luther, 'To the Councilmen of all Cities in Germany That They Establish and Maintain Christian Schools', *Works of Martin Luther* (Philadelphia Edition; Philadelphia: Muhlenberg, 1931) 4:103–130.
5. *Ibid.*, 123.
6. Boyd and King, *Western Education*, 311.
7. See R. White, 'The School in Calvin's Thought and Practice', *JCE* 12 (1969) 5–26.
8. W. Walker, *A History of the Christian Church* (Edinburgh: T. and T. Clark, 1918) 394.
9. Boyd and King, *Western Education*, 200. A certain insularity is evident in the failure to extend this list to the U.S.A., where Calvinist migrants from Europe profoundly affected early educational traditions on the eastern seaboard and had much to do with the strong commitment to democratic education today associated with the U.S.A. See Eavey, *History*, 145.
10. Walker, *History*, 397.
11. Though their initial purpose and mandate was missionary rather than educational. Strategy, however, led them into the establishment of colleges and universities to train leaders and defenders of the faith.
12. See G.N. Vose, 'The Puritans and Education: A Plea for Reassessment', *JCE* 3 (1960) 109–18 and L. Greaves, *The Puritan Revolution and Educational Thought* (New Brunswick: Rutgers University, 1969).
13. Wardle, *Schooled*, 76.
14. *Ibid.*, 90.
15. *Ibid.*, 54.
16. See T.W. Laqueur, *Religion and Respectability: Sunday Schools and Working Class Culture: 1780–1850* (New Haven: Yale University, 1976) 3, 61.
17. *Ibid.*, 23.
18. *Ibid.*, 127, 135.
19. *Ibid.*, 74.
20. *Ibid.*, 45.
21. Eavey, *History*, 234. See also John S. Brubacher, *A History of the Problems of Education*, New York: McGraw-Hill, 2nd ed., 1966, 320ff.
22. Eavey, *History*, 251.
23. Brubacher, *Problems*, 330. In an earlier edition of his book, Brubacher expressed great hopes for this trend. In the present edition, his re-drafted final section is much less assured, and acknowledges some merit in 'evangelical conservative' criticisms that the trend was too naive about man's native goodness.
24. Eavey, *History*, 261.
25. *Ibid.*, 268.
26. I am using this term in the sense it has for Americans, i.e. a view of society which exalts individual freedom to the point where all government regulation is regarded as undesirable. It rests on an Anarchist view of politics and a Romantic view of human nature.
27. I. Illich, *Deschooling Society* (New York: Harper and Row, 1970) xix.
28. *Ibid.*, 40.
29. *Ibid.*, 26.

30. I. Lister, *Deschooling: A Reader* (Cambridge: Cambridge University, 1971) 9. See also K. Collins and P.W. Hughes, *Where Our Junior Secondary Schools are Heading* (Melbourne: ACER, 1982).
31. V. Smith, *Alternatives in Education* (Bloomington, Indiana: Phi Delta Kappa, 1976).
32. In 'Compulsion in Education', *JCE* 52 (1975) 39–57.
33. D. Arnstine, *Philosophy of Education* (New York: Harper and Row, 1967) 232.
34. S. Bowles and H. Gintis, *Schooling in Capitalist America* (London: Routledge and Kegan Paul, 1976) 200.
35. See my "What's 'Open' about Open Education?" in *The Philosophy of Open Education* (ed. David Nyberg; London: Routledge and Kegan Paul, 1975) 3–13.
36. Wardle, *Schooled*, 151.
37. *Ibid*.

4

The Modern Concept of Education

In the previous chapter I discussed two historical movements which, I said, played a crucial part in ushering in the schooled society. One was the Reformation, with its Hebraic insistence on the right of all children to receive an education suited to their capacities, its Hellenistic dependence on professional teachers and formal schooling to provide such an education, and its Medieval fusion of the tasks of general education and faith-nurture. The other was the Industrial Revolution, with its remorseless demand for more knowledge and skills in the workforce, and its consequent secularising effect on social institutions like the school.

In the present chapter I want to examine more closely the phenomenon of secularisation, in particular as it affects the meaning that many people now attach to the term 'education'.[1] I will argue that whereas many Christian people continue to amalgamate the objectives of general education and faith nurture, a body of opinion has developed which sees them as separate tasks calling for the application of different teaching contexts and strategies. While identifying shortcomings in some secular interpretations of the aims of formal education, I will also be urging acceptance of some of the implications as they affect schooling. But I will counsel a very different stance towards the teaching ministries adopted within that faith-community which the Bible calls the body of Christ.

Secularisation

Ask someone what the opposite of 'secular' is and they will probably suggest words like 'religious', 'sacred' or even 'Christian'. The word has had an interesting history. It comes from a Latin word referring to an age or epoch in history. This implies that the opposite notion would be the timeless, eternal, and other-worldly. The word 'secular' therefore came in later centuries to refer to the affairs of everyday life, in contrast to the prime concern of religion (or so it seemed in the Middle Ages) with our immortal destiny in the hereafter. An interesting distinction later emerged in church circles between the 'regular' or 'religious' clergy who entered monastic orders, to loosen their attachment to the attractions of this world, and the 'secular' clergy who lived and worked in ordinary society, though still bound by certain vows not enjoined upon the laity.

These distinctions receive little support from Scripture. There, all believers are called to be 'saints', that is, people set apart from sin to serve God, and this causes them to be at odds with many features of the existing world order (cf. 2 Cor 4:1–6; 6:14–18). But they are not encouraged to opt out of society because of this. Jesus prays that they may be sustained *in* the world, where he has sent them (John 17:14–18), and Paul characterises Christians as Christ's ambassadors, sustaining a reconciling presence in the world (2 Cor 5:16–21). The Jewish philosopher Martin Buber has spoken of 'the hallowing of the everyday':[2] a limpid phrase which cancels out the distinction between the sacred and the secular spheres of life, and reunites personal religion and daily living.

Medieval usage paved the way for people to think of the secular in a yet more radical way. It began to look as though religion did little for ordinary living except hamper discovery and make one feel guilty for enjoying oneself. The world-view or cultural canopy of Christendom which provided the legitimations for all social institutions, from schools and hospitals to prisons and armies, was felt by some thinkers to be oppressive and dispensable. Some of the objectors in this case were dissenting Christians, such as the Separatists and Baptists. Meanwhile, humanist leaders of the fifteenth century Renaissance and the seventeenth century Enlightenment strove to replace the Christian world view with a faith in human nature empowered by rationality.

By the nineteenth century, 'secularists' were understood to be people who wished to withdraw all human activities from the province of religion and base them on logic and scientific method. The legal system would no longer appeal to divine law but to social contract. Social services like hospitals were no longer to be charities motivated by religious compassion but utilities logically demanded by the just state. *Secularism* made man the measure of all things, and trusted that freedom and autonomy would automatically bring out the best in him. Such convictions are articles of faith. Secularism is therefore a life-stance, and one hostile to traditional religion. As such, it offers an alternative canopy for the legitimation of social institutions.

The English 'scientific humanists', who were probably at their strongest just prior to the First World War, were secularists in this sense. Ironically, the most thorough example of a society built on secularist assumptions is probably the communist state, where individual freedom does not extend to questioning the scientific logic of Party policy or tolerating honest dissent.

When we encounter the term *secularisation*, however, it is not usually in reference to the promotion of secularism. Rather, it refers to a social process which has been accelerating since at least the rise of science in the seventeenth century. At that time many forms of enquiry began breaking away from the limited group of older inter-linked disciplines such as philosophy, theology and law. Studies like physics, chemistry, mathematics and engineering developed their own axioms and verification procedures, which could be impartially adopted and used by Christians and non-Christians alike. The church lost the power it had exercised in the time of Copernicus and Galileo to forbid forms of enquiry which appeared to challenge its authority and dogma. And scholarship was the better for it.

The same century saw many struggles for religious freedom, as more people began to realise that the visible church had exceeded its brief by trying to *compel* belief in its teaching.

Lutherans and Calvinists fought Catholics, while Anabaptist and Brethren communities struggled to be free of both. In several countries an aspiration for individual liberty in regard to the expression and practice of one's religious and political opinions led to the development of democratic constitutions.

England's Bill of Rights in 1688 preceded by a century the US Declaration of Independence and the French Declaration of the Rights of Man, but each was a step towards creating a society in which people with different beliefs could live together and find ways of maintaining essential social services. Even before global communications forced us into a pluralistic world community, these former provinces of Christendom were finding ways to protect individual liberty in the multi-faith society. The liberal democratic tradition was born under the canopy of Christendom, with its biblical commitment to the worth of the individual.

In this sense, secularisation does not involve the creation of an alternative anti-religious canopy, but the removal of all such canopies from public institutions. It causes the creation of relatively neutral zones in which citizens of various faiths can meet and maintain the amenities of trade and civilisation. This has often been referred to as the 'privatisation of religion', and undoubtedly it carries with it the danger that religious conviction will be seen as peripheral to the main business of living. But it need not. And it is arguably a better environment in which to evangelise on behalf of the gospel of Christ than one in which compulsion of one sort or another — domestic, educational, legal or military — pushes people into apparent conformity with the Christian life-stance.

The process of secularisation was greatly accelerated by the Industrial Revolution, particularly with respect to the provision of social welfare. Churches, local councils and other charitable bodies found themselves unable to cope with the massive problems of health, education, poor relief and adjustment of the economy which grew in the wake of the social changes caused by the factory system. Increasingly, these responsibilities have come to be borne by the state: responsibilities which have to be carried out impartially and without special favour being shown towards particular religions or social classes.

How ought Christians to react to the process of secularisation? First, they should recognise the extent to which it is a social *fact*, regardless of whether it is considered to be a good or bad thing. There is no turning the clock back to the uni-faith society of Christendom. Modern society is a complex web of public institutions and non-government interest groups. The industrial city accommodates a diversity of activities and allows for a great number of choices of life-style, provided they are consistent with the maintenance of civil order. These are the facts.

It is possible to take the view that secularisation is not only a fact but a good thing. Harvey Cox in *The Secular City*[3] welcomes it as a working out of biblical perspectives, especially with respect to the freedom and responsibility it places on the shoulders of all persons to make what they will of their own lives. Under these conditions, unprotected by customary sanctions and secure traditions, the individual must face the big questions of what meaning he attaches to life and how he proposes to regard his neighbour. Here is a golden opportunity for Christians in free association with such people to commend the Christian option to them.

As so often happens, however, there is also a dark side to the story. Secularisation can also lead to irresponsibility and the breakdown of community, unless minority groups who are concerned with the common good outflank the forces of greed, licence, exploitation and consumerism. One writer has fastened on the sub-title of Cox's book, *The Secular City* — 'a celebration of its liberties and an invitation to its discipline' — and has commented acidly that what we are called to celebrate is:

> The paralysis of power, the breakdown of transportation, the failure of the water supply . . . the decayyof the churches and of public schools, the growth of slums, the exacerbation of ethnic divisions, the heightening of distinctions between rich and poor, the increase in crime, police corruption or police brutality.[4]

Secularisation may present us therefore with both a threat and an opportunity. Christians are not less entitled than any other committed minority group to try to influence policy trends in the media and public institutions. The secular society grants them freedom of worship, speech and assembly which are fruits of the gospel, and will last only as long as the worth of the individual continues to be defended on religious grounds. Christians are therefore challenged to be salt and light in the world, participating in the social process and leavening public institutions with Christian values of compassion and respect for personal integrity and fulfilment.

Those Christians who, fearing contamination, withdraw from encounter with non-Christians in the public domain into ghetto institutions exclusive to their particular brand of Christianity, are passing up this challenge. They should not be surprised if society subsequently becomes more unfeeling and intolerant until, in reaction, evangelists for reform sweep away their liberties in the interests of some new faith canopy, such as Marxism or Islam. In global political terms, the liberal democratic state is a relatively uncommon form of government, constantly threatened by pressures from more totalitarian regimes, whether religious or anti-religious in character.

The Scope of Education

In this changed world, how are we to view the process of education? The question obliges us to make some distinctions. First, 'education' and 'schooling' are not synonymous. On the one hand, we recognise as educational many experiences which do not necessarily take place in school. On the other hand, schools perform a number of functions besides education, such as child-minding, careers advice, and social control.

Secondly, education may be formal or informal. 'Formal education' picks out those times when a person officially recognised as a teacher organises a systematic schedule of learning. The school is indisputably the major agency of formal education in today's society. 'Informal education' identifies those occasions when a person learns things from others who have slipped momentarily, and not always deliberately, into the teaching role while interacting with the learner in a more voluntary context. Such educators can include parents, youth leaders, employers and entertainers.

London philosopher Richard Peters makes some plausible suggestions as to how the idea of education has changed over the centuries.[5] He deduces from a study of dictionary usage that 'education' used to mean everything that went into rearing and training the child. We may say that it was very like the idea of 'nurture', and did not necessarily imply book learning or critical thinking. These latter notions were more likely to apply to the special kind of education offered to the wealthy and the well-born. In such cases one might refer to the education of a 'gentleman', or to a 'liberal' education, involving both schooling and circulation in refined society.

With the coming of industrialism and mass schooling, however, theorists began, according to Peters, to use the term 'education' in a more precise way. Anxious to avoid a heavy emphasis on mere literacy and vocational training, they drew on the Greek idea of the cultivated man, well-rounded in his understanding and able to exercise critical rationality. Consequently, says Peters, the way people spoke of education began to change. It came to be seen as something different from either general nurture or narrow training, in that it focused on the development of the powers of the mind.

In this sense, education sets the individual free from the unreflective customs of his particular social background and home situation. He is able to assess these influences in the light of his wider understanding of the world and the forms of knowledge that have been developed. As his powers of rational evaluation and decision-making increase, he achieves greater self-realisation; he is more an individual person, equipped to cope with the demands of a complex society, and able to obtain pleasure from the pursuit of the more cultured forms of satisfaction.

I think Peters is right in claiming that many people, especially educators themselves, are using the term 'education' in this sense. It reflects two things. One is the social fact of secularisation to which I referred earlier. If we equate Peters' description with what I defined as *formal* education,[6] then we can see how this process has become differentiated from the broader processes of nurture and socialisation.

The school has now become a social institution responsible to the whole community, requiring a secular rationale for its operations. This does not mean that the school necessarily becomes anti-religious. Indeed, if the school neglects to help students attend seriously to the presence and influence of religious ideas in history, literature and contemporary life, then it is open to criticism *on educational grounds*. Equally, if it attends seriously only to one ideological life-stance, be it, say, catholic, calvinist or marxist, then it has again failed to be fully educative. Irrespective of what more particular objectives the sponsors of a particular school or school system may choose to pursue, the modern concept of education itself imposes certain minima which most people accept as valid.

The second characteristic which Peters' analysis reflects is an admiration for Greek rationalism such as we have noted in previous formative eras. Despite his early claims to have been doing a neutral job of spelling out what 'we' *mean* by 'education', Peters has built in a number of his own value preferences, and the general effect is to favour a literary-academic approach which reflects English upper-middle class values. To this extent I would argue he has not adequately represented the expectations of a pluralistic society. The community as a whole expects more of education than Peters does. More recently, Peters has admitted that his analysis is, like everybody else's, unavoidably value-loaded.

To be fair to Peters, he does recognise the value of many of the other things that schools do, and he accepts the need for such activities as counselling, moral training, and instruction in basic skills and vocationally oriented studies. But none of these comes into his definition of education because in his view they are not primarily concerned with 'cognitive transformation', or the development of rational autonomy.[7]

I have argued elsewhere[8] that what people associate with the concept of education includes, but also goes beyond, the achievement of critical rationality. I accept that Peters has shown that critical rationality is *part* of what people generally expect of a rounded education.[9] But I claim that people also agree that education also promotes recognition of the worth and welfare of every person, male and female; the importance of the search for truth in every realm; and the ideal of service to the community. Admittedly these are values to which some ideologies attach less importance than others, which is also true of the commitment to critical rationality. But taken together, they represent the kinds of agreement necessary to maintain an open, multi-faith society. Delete any one of these, and there is a potential threat to liberty.

I do not say that these commitments alone add up to a satisfactory personal life-stance. They are agreements at a practical level, without the underlying reasons or life-meanings which may prompt people to adopt them. They can, however, be a meeting ground for Christian, humanist and, to some extent, marxist, even though the respective world-views of these parties differ greatly. They underlie the secular, democratic societies with which we have become familiar in the western world, and undergird the intrinsic rationales of social institutions like the law-courts, health services and education. Though they fall short of the full-blooded Christian ethic and evangel, they are not incompatible with them, and deserve to be defended and promoted, by Christians, in the name of the general community.

Institutions of formal education have become community meeting places for children and adults from diverse backgrounds, to whom they owe the duties of enlightening the understanding and deepening the commitment to inter-personal goods. With reference particularly to schools, the community expects that the school will tune up, as it were, each individual's capacities — the powers of thinking and feeling — so that all pupils will be better able to survive and find fulfilment in a complex society. This includes attempts to develop not only a critical and well-informed mind, but a finer emotional responsiveness to aesthetic experience and personal relationships. Hence the approach to teaching must be more than literary-academic, as we noted in the previous chapter. Similarly, our reasons for testing achievement must go beyond merely weeding out those of lesser ability and favouring an intellectual elite.

Christian theorists in the *public* domain are well-placed to argue for a richer and more egalitarian concept of formal education than the elitist or consumerist notions currently in vogue. But they must avoid trying to justify their value judgments by appealing to Christian beliefs which the majority do not hold, even if they feel these supply better grounds than the value-rationale of secular-democratic society to which they *may* reasonably appeal.

Christian theorists in the *private* domain, seeking justifications for Christian schools, have problems of an opposite kind. They are free to build their educational theories on more comprehensive views of the world derived from Christian beliefs, but they must then show that what they are doing deserves the title of education in the sense that it provides genuine and honest enlightenment about the nature of the multi-faith society. Are students encouraged to examine critically both the faith-basis of the community of commitment which is sponsoring their own school, and the ideologies of their neighbours in the multi-faith society? If not, and given the compulsory character of schooling discussed in the previous chapter, they are not being educated but indoctrinated.

The Concept of Christian Education

If then the concept of education has become attached to one of the processes of socialisation in a multi-faith society, and is regarded as referring to the (relatively) neutral business of expanding human awareness and capacities, rather than to fixing certain beliefs and behaviours in the captive learner, how does this meaning then modify any other concept that is bracketed with it? Specifically, what can it mean to speak of 'Christian education'?

There are many words which combine comfortably with 'education'. We are fairly clear what we are talking about when we speak of language education, science education or political education. The secular meaning of education tells us that we are seeking to make the learner more skilled and aware of the issues in each of the areas of experience identified by these respective adjectives.

There are other combinations which seem either clumsy or totally inappropriate. 'Driver education' seems a rather inflated way of referring to a limited range of mainly practical studies which might more appropriately be called 'driver training'. 'Plant education' now seems quite odd, though three hundred years ago it would have been an acceptable usage. Plant growth can be directed, animals can be trained. But though humans too can be directed and trained, in speaking of education in current discourse we seem to be focusing on a higher level of functioning, involving the conscious mind and emotions.

To which category of possibilities does 'Christian education' belong? When we refer to Christianity we are denoting a life-style or world-view based on distinctive beliefs and values. Since all intelligent people don't automatically accept the claim that these beliefs and values are true, 'Christian' must refer to a preferred ideology, one committed position amongst several possibilities. So 'Christian education' could mean one of two things.

First, it could mean making the learner more critically aware of the ideas and institutions of Christianity, just as political education makes the learner more aware of political processes. This would allow the two words to be bracketed, but two objections arise. One is that it is rather unusual to pick out one example in the general area of 'religious education' and identify it in this way. We would then have to do the same for each other ideology investigated in this general area of study. That would be very clumsy. We just don't talk about segments of subject matter in that way.[10]

The second objection is even more fatal. Most users of the phrase 'Christian education' don't mean merely teaching *about* Christianity; they mean teaching *for* Christian commitment. Strictly speaking, if the two words are being bracketed to give this sense, then the result is internally contradictory. If one is teaching for Christian commitment in the context of compulsory classroom instruction, then indoctrination (and the violation of individual rights) is occurring. If one is teaching for Christian commitment in a voluntary context, then one is engaged in evangelism. Neither activity is properly described as education.

Nevertheless, the phrase 'Christian education' is frequently given this second meaning of 'teaching for commitment to the

Christian way'. Where it is then applied to the curriculum of a Christian-sponsored school, it obliges us to raise questions about the legitimacy of that institution's claim to be providing a validly educational experience. Where it is used in church circles to describe the Sunday school programme, it generates ambiguity about what precisely the teachers are trying to do: present the documents of faith factually? invite critical examination of the belief claims of Christianity? socialise the learners into the church community? or persuade them into an expression of commitment to Christ? It is not unreasonable to suggest that the oft-noted fall-out from Sunday school of youngsters entering the teen years is due in large part to the resentment they feel at being pressured by a faith wearing the authority-trappings of the schooling model they are compelled to endure on weekdays.

There is another risk involved in assigning certain of the church's activities to the category of something called Christian education. They may tend to develop a life of their own, artificially divorced from other categories of activity such as worship and mission. This is because the word 'education' invites people to draw the analogy with the self-justifying institution of formal education in the secular society.

But the teaching ministries within a faith-community are not self-justifying. They are meant to provide the data-base for evangelistic proclamation, intelligent worship, growth in grace, and witness in society. We learn more about our faith in order not merely to enlarge our minds but to improve our living. The paraphernalia of courses and certificates in Christian education can easily become a substitute for active service; a protracted preparation for a testimony which never has time to leave the Christian ghetto.

Consider worship. There is a tendency to identify the church's worship solely with the all-age 'Sunday service of worship'. This fosters two errors. One is that of regarding worship as a stylised activity built around specially furnished premises, mood music, or rituals focused on clerical regality. This can easily substitute a fondling of the emotions for that discovery of new truth about God which sets the heart aflame with intelligent praise. An excessive interest in liturgy and religious aesthetics is often a sign of a loss of confidence in the reliability and accuracy of revealed truth. True worship is fired by experiences of God's mercy during the daily round and discoveries of his good purpose as a result of studying life in the light of Scripture. Only when the people of God share these findings with each other does spectator worship turn into participant worship.

The second error is to deny to group activities in the church other than 'services of worship' the right to be viewed as occasions for worship. A task-force engaged in, say, an action project to help single parents in the neighbourhood meets to plan and review its activities. The group has just had particular success in relieving a tense situation, and falls to praising God in prayer. The believers are at worship. In discussing how they will next proceed, they look for spiritual guidelines in the Scriptures. They are at study. They then move out again to embrace their needy neighbours. They are at mission. Church programmes which fail to reflect this cycle of learning, praising and serving are not worthy to be called Christian.

With regard, again, to mission, the schooling model tempts us to 'have our lesson', and then leave it to other parts of the church's programme to encourage the learners to apply the truths learnt to the life lived. Or else it prompts us to design 'projects', associated with the educational objectives of the lesson rather than the spiritual motivations of the individual to help his neighbour. Teachers in secular schools all too rarely invite their pupils to engage in forms of community action deriving from their studies, but even when they do, problems of motivation arise because the projects generated tend to be viewed as assessment-related chores rather than as voluntarily embraced outcomes of learning. The secular concept of education focuses on *enlightenment*; the church's teaching ministries aim *by* enlightenment to trigger *commitment* to God in worship and the neighbour in mission. They are instrumental to higher objectives.

In short, the term 'Christian education' is a handicap to clear thinking about the teaching ministries of the church. A final demonstration of this point is the encouragement it gives to critics of the church to charge Christians with indoctrination, coupled with the willingness of some Christians to equate evangelism with indoctrination.

Indoctrination and Evangelism

The Oxford dictionary supplies for 'indoctrination' the literal meaning of implanting a doctrine by teaching.[11] Understood in this way, the term is clear and unobjectionable. In previous centuries it was used as a term descriptive of instruction in religious beliefs, without any suggestion that this was in any way a discreditable thing to do. But, as we have seen in the case of the word 'education', meanings can change over time. At the present time, to say that someone is indoctrinating someone else is to accuse him of malpractice as a teacher. How has this stigma been acquired?

Doctrines are beliefs and explanations which, while helping us to make sense of some aspect of life, are not in themselves provable by scientific means. In a uni-faith society like medieval Christendom, the basic assumptions and claims of Christianity were taken for granted; they constituted a canopy of meaning which imparted sense to all the activities which went on beneath it. But once society became the secularised host to many minority groups with different belief systems, and once the state became obliged to provide universal education, an understandable sensitivity developed towards the teaching of disputed doctrines as though they were unassailable truths.

It is unfortunate that at the very time when governments were searching for acceptably impartial ways of educating children to cope with their societies, many bitter and unlovely arguments were going on about the control of education, not only between Christians and non-Christians but amongst the Christian denominations themselves. The tendency was for governments to wash their hands of such disputes and to prescribe curricula which either left controversial areas like religion, morality and politics out altogether, or which gave them grudging admission under conditions (such as non-assessment) different from other subjects.

Increasingly, however, dissatisfaction has grown with the

value-vacuum this creates in so many areas of the curriculum, and one reaction has been to press for a more deliberate effort to make children *aware* of the value dimensions of life through the study of belief systems. It should be noted, however, that this effort has been defined and argued in secular terms. Children are to be taught *about* religions, not persuaded *into* one by slanted teaching. The concept of *education* requires that they be made more aware of the cultural impact of religious (and moral and political) belief systems in the history and present functioning of society, and that they be encouraged to think about them critically with a view to taking the religious dimension seriously enough to make an informed personal choice amongst the options available to them.

By contrast, *indoctrination* has come to be regarded as the attempt to fix certain beliefs in the minds of learners without making them aware of the dissentient views held by others in their community, and without equipping them to examine the evidence for themselves. This is not the same as *conditioning*, which bypasses the conscious mind and will, for it does invite students to use their minds to study and embrace the beliefs involved. But like horses held to the chosen path by reins and blinkers, they are not allowed to see what their serious options are, and they are likely to be deceived as to the comparative strength of the value-claims set before them.

There are sincere Christians whose concern for the eternal welfare of their students and children is so great that they would rather bring them into the kingdom of God like hobbled horses than risk the bad choice that might result from letting them choose for or against God on the fullest evidence available. One can sympathise with their concern, but not their low estimate of human responsibility. We cannot excuse teaching methods that are not far in spirit from the coercion used by the medieval Inquisition. As was noted in chapter two, such abuses of personal freedom are entirely alien to Jesus' way of dealing with people.

Indoctrination is sub-Christian wherever it occurs. In chapter three we distinguished between two types of learning environment: the compulsory and the voluntary. Each type can be abused through indoctrinative teaching.

The compulsory curriculum of the day school can only be justified if the end in view is education: the enlargement of personal awareness and the capacity to choose responsibly. If that curriculum is warped by the special interests of a particular minority group, to the point where it does not give fair treatment to other persuasive life-stances — whether by a distorted choice of subject matter or by the teacher's use of personal influence to impose his own life-stance on the pupils — then what is being attempted is indoctrination, not education.

The second kind of learning environment arises in the voluntary group. We said in chapter three that here the 'rules of the game' are different because both teachers and learners have available to them freedoms not present in the environment of compulsory education. The teacher is free to commend his own life-stance; the learner is free to take it or leave it, to listen or to refuse to listen. But even in these circumstances, evangelism can degenerate into indoctrination.

Evangelism involves information and invitation. The information we are to pass on is the salvation-history revealed in the Bible, and in particular the events and interpretations surrounding the person of Christ. The invitation we make is to count the cost, repent and believe the good news by acting on it. Counting the cost involves weighing up both the intellectual and moral consequences of commitment.

There are evangelists who hide the strenuous demands of denying self, embracing suffering, and following Christ through thick and thin. They offer roses without the thorns, peace without perseverance, joy without pain. Such misrepresentation is a foul betrayal of the Master's call. Other evangelists studiously avoid the hard questions and recite a neat doctrinal package accompanied by the demand that no doubts be entertained. Doubting is sin, belief is absolute and can only be weakened by reasons. These are the indoctrinators, substituting fanaticism for faith.

It is because so many evangelists have preferred indoctrination to reasoned persuasion that many people have rejected the faith and felt bitter about the confidence tricks attempted upon them. It is also the reason why some writers equate evangelism with indoctrination and disapprove of any attempt to persuade others to change their beliefs, even in a free encounter. But taken to a logical extreme this view would create the absurd situation where nobody ever recommended anything to anybody, or warned another about errors in his belief.

True evangelism works from the same premise as good education: that other people are individuals with worth, rights, needs, and the capacity to consider reasonably the claims and evidence that others set before them. There are no allowable short cuts. Learners and hearers are not to be stampeded into decisions not truly their own, nor manipulated psychologically to mouth the responses that are considered desirable, without necessarily understanding what they are saying.

Christian Nurture

If the term 'Christian education' is so productive of misunderstanding, how else shall we characterise the teaching ministries of the Christian community of believers? One candidate enjoying a recent revival in usage is 'Christian nurture'. This term has both a great strength and an important weakness. Its strength is that it implies a more intimate and whole-person approach to up-bringing, coming as it does from the warm word 'nourish', than the modern concept of education. The weakness is that it is associated mainly with early child-rearing and sounds protectionist, as if the learner is to be shielded from risky encounter with the world beyond the family nest.

Linguistic considerations aside, a more fundamental theological debate lies beneath the surface of this notion. Views of how to regard learners in the Christian body range along a continuum from what I will call the decisional to the developmental.

The *decisional* view hinges on a conviction that each individual stands in radically different relation to God, persons and the world before and after conversion. Conversion is regarded as an identifiable point in every person's conscious experience. Before this point, the individual is a rebel under God's judgment, incapable of right spiritual thought or action. After conversion, he or she is a child of God through grace, able to understand the things of the spirit.

This view makes evangelism a rather magical affair, where, by the recitation of biblical cue-words and texts, the evangelist jolts the hearer into a faith-response towards Jesus. Verbal affirmation of repentance from sin and trust towards God is regarded as the necessary and sufficient outward sign that the person has passed from death to life, and may now be taught the deeper things of God.

The approach can be almost cruel towards children. Since they are regarded as lost in sin until they consciously affirm faith, they are likely to be pestered to make suitable verbal professions so that they will then qualify for more systematic teaching. This kind of child evangelism seems easy because it is not difficult to persuade children to make the desired responses. It is another question, however, whether those responses represent mere external conformity or meaningfully reflect deep inner change.

Some forms of aggressive child evangelism elicit 'decisions' from the same children over and over again. This may be good for statistics, but not for discipleship. The emphasis is all on the verbal, and the maturing adolescent is likely to remember such experiences either with embarrassment or tolerant amusement. 'When I was a child, I talked like a child . . . When I became a man, I put childish ways behind me' (1 Cor 13:11). The religious enthusiasm of childhood has been dismissed as a thing of the moment.

The *developmental* view hinges on a conviction that religious faith develops by degrees, and is not to be thought of as a quantum leap from unbelief into faith, but as a gradual deepening of one's response to the God who loved us before we knew him, and performed his saving act on our behalf before we ever sought his help. Spiritual nurture is therefore to be thought of as a steady growth in grace aided by teaching about the faith and its implications.

For those who strive to be fully biblical in their justifications, the developmental approach needs some further qualifications than this. Beginning with the spiritual condition of the child, developmental theorists argue that infants and young children, though identified with the fallen human species in their natures, are accepted by God until they reach an age at which they are able to affirm allegiance to him for themselves. Since outside observers cannot observe their inner spiritual state and standing, their task is to build up the child's knowledge of God and experience of Christian body-life so that personal faith will spring up almost imperceptibly, seemingly like any other expected attainment of maturation. An oft-quoted passage from Horace Bushnell's *Christian Nurture* represents the position well:

> What is the true idea of Christian education? . . . *That the child is to grow up a Christian, and never know himself as being otherwise.* In other words, the aim, effort, and expectation should be, not, as is commonly assumed, that the child is to grow up in sin, to be converted after he comes to a mature age; but that he is to open on the world as one that is spiritually renewed, not remembering the time when he went through a technical experience, but seeming rather to have loved what is good from his earliest years.[12]

Liberal Christian theorists in the United States acclaim Bushnell as 'the father of the Christian education movement' in that country, and his stance has encouraged many religious education theorists to draw heavily on secular developmental ideas and research. In an appreciative comment, Catholic theorist Thomas Groome calls Bushnell's approach a 'socialisation model' of Christian education. He also places John Westerhoff III, current editor of the R.E.A. journal *Religious Education*, in the same tradition.[13] This is somewhat less than fair to Westerhoff, who has discussed conversion in terms which take him beyond Bushnell or Groome,[14] and who represents a mediating position to which we shall return in a moment.

Well before religious theorists began to take an interest in the developmental studies of psychologists, however, there existed a theory of progressive spiritual socialisation which grew out of the catechetical practices of the early church. It was noted in chapter two that catechumenal schools were designed for the instruction of new converts to faith. Naturally enough, the catechumens had to be old enough to understand the teaching, and were generally adults. As time went on, however, the canopy of Christendom obscured the difference between the indifferent and the personally committed, and it came to be assumed that all were Christians provided they had submitted to the rituals of the church.

The first ritual was baptism. Therefore children were at risk if caused to wait until the age when they could become catechumens. Hence the long-standing Catholic policy has been to baptise children as soon after birth as possible, to ensure their inclusion in the body of Christ. We have seen that this doctrine of baptismal regeneration tended to work against the practice of instructing children and ordinary people in matters of faith, at least until the Counter-reformation. From that time on *catechesis*, or instruction in Christian beliefs, was given more prominence in Catholic church schools, and the term is still widely used in Catholic circles.

R.M. Rummery, a De La Salle brother in Melbourne, has usefully spelled out the distinction between religious education — understood as 'teaching about' (as in secular education) — and catechesis. The aim of catechesis, he says, is 'to develop the faith received in Baptism at the various stages of life.'[15] It is a task to be performed within the church. Here is a recognition of the distinctness of the spheres of general education for survival in a multi-faith society, and teaching for commitment within the community of believers. But Rummery's theory remains in a traditional frame to the extent that he relates both operations to the work of the Catholic school.

The chief shortcoming of developmental or socialisation approaches is that they tend to pin all their hopes on instruction within a Christian community and to have difficulties with the concept of evangelism. Another familiar Catholic term is 'Christian formation', suggesting the moulding of character by surrounding the learner with a carefully monitored environment of church related influences. Home, church and church-school together fill the hours of the child's day with Christian symbols, rites and authority figures. It is a picture very suggestive of both conditioning and indoctrination.

Thomas Groome tries to guard against such charges by expounding an approach called 'Christian religious education'. As part of his explanation of why he chose so cumbersome a label, he embraces the sense conveyed by the word 'education' of 'enabling people to deal critically and creatively with their social reality, rather than simply fitting them into it.'[16] He then goes on to define catechesis as 'the activity of reechoing or retelling the story of Christian faith that has been handed down.'[17] These definitions set catechesis as one essential type of teaching activity within the larger programme of Christian religious education.

This is a valuable differentiation, similar to the one I have been trying to make between the secular task of education (in religion, science, history, etc.) and the teaching ministries of the believing community. But Groome has not emancipated himself from the schooling model with its overtone of compulsion. Nor has he an effective strategy for evangelism of those outside the church. It doesn't fit his model.

Westerhoff has moved beyond Groome both in his attempts to accommodate the phenomenon of conversion in his model, which I touched on earlier, and in his declaration in 1976 that the church must shake itself free of the 'schooling-instruction paradigm'.[18] In both respects I am in sympathy with him. If I draw back from embracing his emphasis on a 'community of faith-enculturation paradigm'[19] as the new direction in which to go, it is because I detect in it a greater reliance on the authority of the church than on the authority of Scripture. In particular, Westerhoff neglects the oft-documented capacity of the word of Scripture alone to lead people into saving faith even before they have encountered people of faith.

One of the strategies on which Westerhoff lays great stress, for example, is the use of liturgy and ritual as a teaching medium. 'Christian education', he says, 'should be related to preparation for these rituals.'[20] It is doubtful if any of the rituals he lists are clearly biblical in intention. Though he uses biblical names for some of them, they look more like 'rites of passage' adapted from anthropological descriptions of rituals used in tribal societies to keep the clan together.

What Point Have We Reached?

As we approach the half-way mark of the book and the completion of our ground-clearing exercise, it may be helpful to ask what point has been reached. I began this study by noting in chapter one that there are many ambiguities and confusions in the way people speak of Christian education. In an effort to locate the causes of this confusion, I looked first at the Greek and biblical legacies, noting several differences between them. In the later part of chapter two I noted the attempts to amalgamate these two traditions in a medieval synthesis which gave rise to many of the notions which are still with us today.

Some of these traditions have persisted into the modern era despite the Reformation emphasis on getting back to NT values, and account for such ideas as professionalised teaching, schools as the main medium of education, and compulsory attendance. I also noted in chapter three that the effects of the industrial revolution were to hasten and universalise such developments. At the present time, however, schools are coming under criticism from several quarters, and I drew on some of these criticisms to highlight essential differences between education for enlightenment and teaching for commitment.

My argument in the present chapter has been that the development of a secular ideal of a general education for all, emphasising skills of social survival, critical rationality and a commitment to the welfare of persons in community has been a good thing. Any good school, public or Christian, will strive to attain it. But I have also argued that we need to return to a more biblical idea of teaching to understand how different and complementary to education should be the church's programme of teaching and learning. It is time we 'deschooled Christianity'.[21]

In the last few sections I have examined some of the more recent attempts to remodel such concepts as 'Christian education' and 'Christian nurture' and found them inadequate at various points. It is time to move beyond criticism to reconstruction. In the next chapter I begin the task of rebuilding our perception of the teaching ministries of the gathered faith community, and of giving examples of structures which more adequately reflect biblical perspectives.

Footnotes

1. An earlier and somewhat different critique of secularisation appeared in chapter one of my book *Called to Teach*.
2. M. Buber, *I and Thou* (trans. R.G. Smith; New York: Scriveners, 1958) 87–89.
3. *The Secular City* (Harmondsworth: Penguin, 1968).
4. R.E. Fitch, 'The Protestant Sickness', quoted in *The Situation Ethics Debate* (ed. H. Cox; Philadelphia: Westminster, 1968) 120.
5. In chapter two (which presents a revised version of an earlier article by Peters) of P.H. Hirst and R.S. Peters, *The Logic of Education* (London: Routledge and Kegan Paul, 1970).
6. Peters' analysis suffers from the failure to make the formal/informal distinction. Hence we are tempted to translate all his injunctions into the schooling mode, and to interpret schooling itself as being mainly devoted to an astringent academic-rational objective. This has a limiting effect on discussions of the concepts both of education and schooling.
7. To this extent, Peters does distinguish the more specific task of education from the broader responsibilities of schooling. But he does not go the other way and explicate forms of education beyond the school, chiefly because his intellectualist concept of education only works under formal tuition, cf. R.S. Peters, 'Democratic Values and Educational Aims', *Teacher's College Record* 80 (February 1979) 465.
8. See my 'Education for Commitment: A Logical Contradiction?' *JET* 15 (1981) 159–70.
9. Though some people are afraid of it. They want the school to produce conformists, not critics. No Christian should fear critical rationality, for Jesus sought to awaken it so that would-be followers knew clearly what they were getting into before they decided to join him. (see page 36).
10. Though it must be admitted that one state, Western Australia, allows a junior high school elective to be called 'Christian education' (it were better called 'Study of Christianity') and another, Queensland, requires what it calls 'religious instruction' to be confined to the study of Christianity.
11. There is a useful body of analytic writing on the concept of indoctrination, amongst which I specially recommend J. Kleinig, 'Educating and Indoctrinating' in *Concepts of Education* (ed. J.V. d'Cruz and P.J. Sheehan; Melbourne: Dove Communications, 1976) 23–31 and I.A. Snook, ed., *Concepts of Indoctrination* (London: Routledge and Kegan Paul, 1972).
12. H. Bushnell, *Christian Nurture* (Grand Rapids: Baker, 1979) 10.
13. T.H. Groome, *Christian Religious Education* (Melbourne: Dove, 1980) 116–20.
14. See J.H. Westerhoff III, *Will Our Children Have Faith?* (Melbourne: Dove, 1976) 35–41.
15. R.M. Rummery, *Catechesis and Religious Education in a Pluralist Society* (Sydney: Dwyer, 1975) 166.
16. Groome, *Christian*, 15. Groome pays tribute to John Dewey and Paulo Freire for this criterion, Had he known R.S. Peters, his would also have been a very appropriate name to add in relation to this criterion.
17. *Ibid.*, 27.
18. Westerhoff, *Children*, 11. My own first complaint against the schooling model was in 1971, in *Called to Teach*, esp. chaps. 3 and 8.
19. *Ibid.*, 50.
20. *Ibid.*, 59.
21. *Idem*, 'Deschooled,' 5–21.

Part B

TEACHING IN TODAY'S CHURCH

5

Teaching for Commitment

The key concept in our reconstruction is commitment. People sometimes speak as though commitment *precedes* belief; they imply that it involves a leap in the dark, an arbitrary gesture *after* which it becomes possible to believe things which were previously thought to be either untrue or implausible. But the word 'commitment' demands an object — commitment *to* what? Thus philosopher Roger Trigg argues that commitment is 'acting in accordance with a belief.'[1] We commit ourselves to some person, cause or idea because of some prior belief, however minimal in content, that the object of commitment is true and worthy.

Christian commitment is not blind. A non-believer encounters evidence of some kind which prompts him to take seriously the claims of Christ. The evidence may be found in the quality of a Christian friend's life, or in an active proclamation of some part of the Christian salvation story. The non-believer's thinking is challenged, and he begins to believe that God is, and that Jesus was telling the truth about himself. But this does not make the new believer a Christian. As the apostle James wryly points out, even the demons believe that there is one God. But all that their belief does for them is to make them shudder (Js 2:19). To become a Christian requires that one act on the belief and submit one's personality to the living God.

This distinction is sometimes characterised as the difference between head-knowledge or belief *about*, and heart's-desire or belief *in*. To avoid confusion, I am characterising the second as commitment. Actually, I would like to go beyond Trigg's definition and say that commitment in this sense is a *disposition* to act in accordance with one's beliefs.

This implies two things: first, that Christian commitment is not just a momentary choice or a passing desire but a settled tendency in the personality, as much maintained by the will as by the mind and emotions. Secondly, our Christian commitment is sometimes betrayed by the individual choices we make. When we do what in our best moments we don't want to do, as Paul describes it in Romans 7:15, this is a lapse for which we need to seek forgiveness; it is not a reversal of commitment. 'It is no longer I myself who do it,' says Paul, 'but it is sin living in me.' In other words, my commitment is my willed tendency to affirm Christ in my life. I now regard this as the real me, and I regard my sins not as expressions of a contrary commitment, but as throwbacks to a 'me' I no longer believe in.

Changing Commitment

Christian commitment is not blind. It derives from something I believe. I cannot be said to believe something which I actually know to be false or silly. I must suppose that my belief has some kind of plausibility; my mind must give consent. That is why forms of evangelism which try to stampede people (including children) into verbal profession of faith without engaging their reason fail to awaken commitment. At best they can guarantee only parroted belief or conditioned conformity.

Non-Christians sometimes claim that Christian beliefs only make sense to those who have made the leap of faith and arbitrarily affirmed the existence of God in Christ. If that were the case, then everybody's personal life-stance, whether Christian, marxist, Muslim, scientific humanist, or whatever, would have to be viewed as an irrational leap, no more or less valid than anyone else's. But such commitments always have a sub-stratum of belief which can be subjected to investigation, and though it is never possible to obtain clinching proof that a particular life-view is the one true account of reality, it is feasible to compare its degree of plausibility and comprehensiveness with others.

The invitation to consider the reasonableness of the Christian view of the world is present in all honourable evangelism. From the prophets to the apostles, the testimony challenges its hearers to consider, weigh up, reason together, come and see, inspect and test. This message was not 'done in a corner', as Paul puts it in appealing to King Agrippa's will *and mind*, but is 'true and reasonable' (Acts 26:25–26). Agrippa recognises that Paul is trying to *persuade* him, not frighten or awe him into the kingdom, and he breaks off the dialogue because, indeed, he is finding it too persuasive.

Many others, of course, recognised the reasonableness of the apostle's message and were converted. What happened to them? First, they were persuaded in their minds. The foundations of their beliefs were shaken up. Admittedly, miraculous external events sometimes helped to shake them, as when Peter healed the cripple at the temple gate and Paul calmed his gaoler during an earthquake. But the first reaction of those involved was to ask what these events *meant*, so that thought preceded commitment, by however small a degree. Secondly came the response of will, a resolve to live in accordance with their new beliefs; they committed themselves to the Way.

Thirdly, they looked for a community of believers who were similarly committed. Christian beliefs cannot be privatised, because they make reality claims which are bigger than our personal subjectivities. The gospel does not merely offer people a psychological crutch (though peace of mind is one of the wonderful by-products) but a way to come to terms with objective reality. The meaning of the cosmos resides in the purpose of the Creator, and getting right with God corrects warps in our understanding of ourselves, other persons, and nature. Therefore we are moved to share what we know with others, in hopes of improving our grasp of the truth that liberates. Fellowship is built not just on common feelings but on agreed belief and a common resolve to serve the Lord, just as evangelism involves not only an offer of inner peace and purpose but a set of truth-claims about God and the world.

Teaching and Commitment

To hold beliefs requires that we understand them and can fit them into our general awareness of the world. To express commitment in ways consistent with our beliefs requires understanding also. Many church people assent glibly to creeds and confessions without exhibiting the kinds of behaviour implied by such beliefs. As often as not, such inconsistency results not from wilful disobedience but from ignorance or intellectual laziness. Their experience of church frequently fails to provide that stimulus to learn more about the Christian walk which is a typical feature of a true community of commitment.

Our first model for such a community is the nation of Israel at its best. As we saw in chapter two, Judaism centred on a teaching God, who expected of his people a life-style consistent with the law he had revealed to them. Moral and spiritual teaching were built in to family activities, and seasonal celebrations. The famous Psalm 119 reiterates in scores of ways the dependence of deep commitment on understanding.

The NT provides our second and fuller model, revealing the gathered congregation of believers as a learning environment in which each one teaches the other, and all learn from each other. In chapter four we saw that both worship and witness are energised by a well-taught understanding. Christian faith-communities grow in faith and action through their teaching ministries. The content of such teaching is not religious education in the general sense; it is the recital and study of the salvation story presented in the Scriptures. Telling this story is both an invitation to commitment and an illumination of the committed life-style. Studying the story objectively in the classroom is one thing; telling it within the voluntary community of commitment is quite another. Those who enter this community, whether as enquirers or full participants, come of their own free will to hear the proclamation. There is no ambiguity about its truth claims. This community has been raised up by those who have embraced its beliefs as true, and the community itself is, at best, a living demonstration of the life-style such beliefs generate.

Theologically, the standing of persons before God is determined by each individual's fundamental disposition, whether it is self-ward or God-ward. The self-centred individual needs converting; the God-oriented person needs strengthening in awareness and resolve. On the face of it, this creates a number of problems for the teacher in the church.

How, for example, is one to know whether evangelism or nurture is called for in the particular case? On a decisional teaching model, this question is crucial, especially, as we saw in the previous chapter, in the case of children. Conversely, if one favours a developmental model, how does one know when to expect the great, life-changing commitment? Does it imply a change in teaching procedures at that point?

If we raise questions in this form, then a lot depends on our ability to identify where individuals stand in relation to God. We noted earlier that verbal profession may well be superficial, especially in the case of children; and some who profess Christian commitment have on occasions done so to deceive. Heeding Jesus' 'by their fruits' we may try to infer a person's commitment from his behaviour, but we can often be wrong about that too.

But the real problem here lies in the way we are posing the pedagogic question. Suppose we frame it in another way and ask: how do we teach for commitment?

Two things now become apparent. The first is that both evangelism before conversion and Christian nurture after conversion involve teaching for commitment. Each strives to build, on whatever present understanding the individual already has, a fuller awareness of God and his ways. Furthermore, the intention of such teaching is to evoke a response, to invite action on the beliefs presented.

The second point is that the commitment or whole-self disposition we have been discussing is built on a host of subsidiary beliefs and commitments, and on daily renewals of our primary commitment to God. In eternal perspective, our turning to God is decisively once-for-all; in the flow of time we may not be entirely sure ourselves when it occurred (and theological differences abound on this issue), but we reaffirm it constantly in moments of joy, repentance, temptation and triumph. And we don't always reaffirm it in the same words or actions. Seeing a wonder of nature, we reaffirm it by giving glory to God. Under suffering we reaffirm it by clinging stubbornly to our belief in his good purpose. Repenting of sin, we reaffirm it by asking his forgiveness. Seeing someone in need, we reaffirm it by offering help in his name.

Such considerations enable us to chart the way ahead for teachers in the faith community. They are to regard themselves as teaching for commitment. This is not something to be done mechanically or by formula. If the content is the salvation-story, represented in a host of ways by the Scriptural record, then our central method will be to familiarise our hearers with that record. Since it is typical of the record that our response to God is illustrated in many ways, it will be appropriate to invite responses of many kinds from each other.

For example, in learning of Jacob's responses to the God of his fathers, we see a gradual purging of his initial self-centred bargaining spirit. David, realising his guilt, expresses his true sorrow to God and asks to be cleansed and restored. A boy is invited to donate his lunch to the preacher Jesus. James criticises those who show special favour to the rich and powerful. Constantly, the great story invites responses of similar kinds from the readers. So will we, the teachers. To this extent our model is decisional, but it is not restricted in focus to the mystically decisive moment when the soul passes from death to life. Hence the same act of teaching for commitment may have for some an evangelistic appeal while being for others a reinforcement of a commitment already embraced.

This also charts the way ahead for our ministry to children. Irrespective of the resolution of the theological controversy as to whether children are sinners till they consciously turn to God, or children of God until they consciously turn away,[2] our task remains the same. We are to tell the salvation story by a balanced sampling of Scripture geared to their level of understanding at the time. In this task we will welcome the insights psychologists can give us into how they perceive, think and feel at various ages. Also, wherever the portion of the great story we are dealing with illustrates how we can be responsive to God, we will invite the children to respond in like manner at their own level.

It will not trouble us that children's responses are often of short duration, nor, conversely, will we be nonplussed to find that some children are capable at a very young age of turning to God in a fundamental and enduring sense. Either way, beliefs will be clarified and the disposition to be God's person strengthened.

To this extent our teaching model will therefore also be developmental, but it will be directed towards a developing commitment, not merely a developing awareness. Nevertheless, it must *include* a developing awareness. In the light of the Christian objections raised in the previous chapter to indoctrination, we will have a responsibility to ensure that older children are given the opportunity to examine their own beliefs critically and to understand that they live not by knowledge but by reasonable faith. In a multi-faith society they need to become intelligently aware of other faith claims that they will encounter, and the light which the Bible sheds on these.[3]

Developmentally speaking, adolescence is the ideal time to invite the learner to examine what has been learnt and hitherto accepted in somewhat piecemeal fashion, and to 'get it all together' in mind and will. It is the time for the individual to grasp Christianity as a world-view, and to decide whether to embrace it as the home of the spirit. Westerhoff speaks of a passage from 'faith given (through nurture)' to 'faith owned'.[4]

But Westerhoff's view works best with the children of Christian parents; less effectively for the non-churched and others 'born out of due season'. For them the teaching which will be of most help — given that they will probably have encountered many contrary beliefs and world-views already at home or elsewhere in the pluralistic society — will be the persuasive proclamation of the central Christian story. Yet even here, our presentation will not be in the spirit of 'Here is our mystery. Take it or leave it', but rather 'Here is our story. Examine it and see how it fits the world you experience'. Awareness is the herald of commitment.

The key to *what* we teach lies not in theological guesses as to whether our hearers are converted or not but in estimates of how much acquaintance they already have with the Christian story. Paul's point of entry with Greeks in Athens was different from those which he adopted with Jews in Jerusalem and Christians in Ephesus (Acts 17:16–31; 20:18–35; 22:1–21). But always he preached for greater awareness and deeper commitment. He started at his hearers' level of consciousness and sought to lead them further in to the centre of God's will for them, by reasoned argument and admonition.

The Curriculum Process

We are now in a position to see just how useful are current curriculum approaches in general educational theory.[5] Many of the systematic syllabuses devised for use in Sunday schools and Christian education programmes draw heavily on curriculum models developed in secular settings. We may summarise much writing on the curriculum process by expounding diagram 5.1: The Curriculum Process.

In this diagram, the curriculum cycle lies upon a larger social background which supplies the general goals and values of education. These are conditioned by social expectations, ethical considerations and the findings of psychology. *Social expectations* require us to take account of what people are used to, the institutions they have inherited, and the expectations they have of roles such as pupil and teacher. *Ethical considerations* relate to our understanding of what it is legitimate to attempt in the compulsory classroom, what rights children have, and how much of a value consensus operates in the public domain. *Psychological findings* enable us to pace our teaching to the pupil's stage of development and to make our methods more effective.

All these considerations provide a canopy of beliefs and values under which the more day-to-day operations of the curriculum process function. From time to time a major shift in

Diagram 5.1 THE CURRICULUM PROCESS

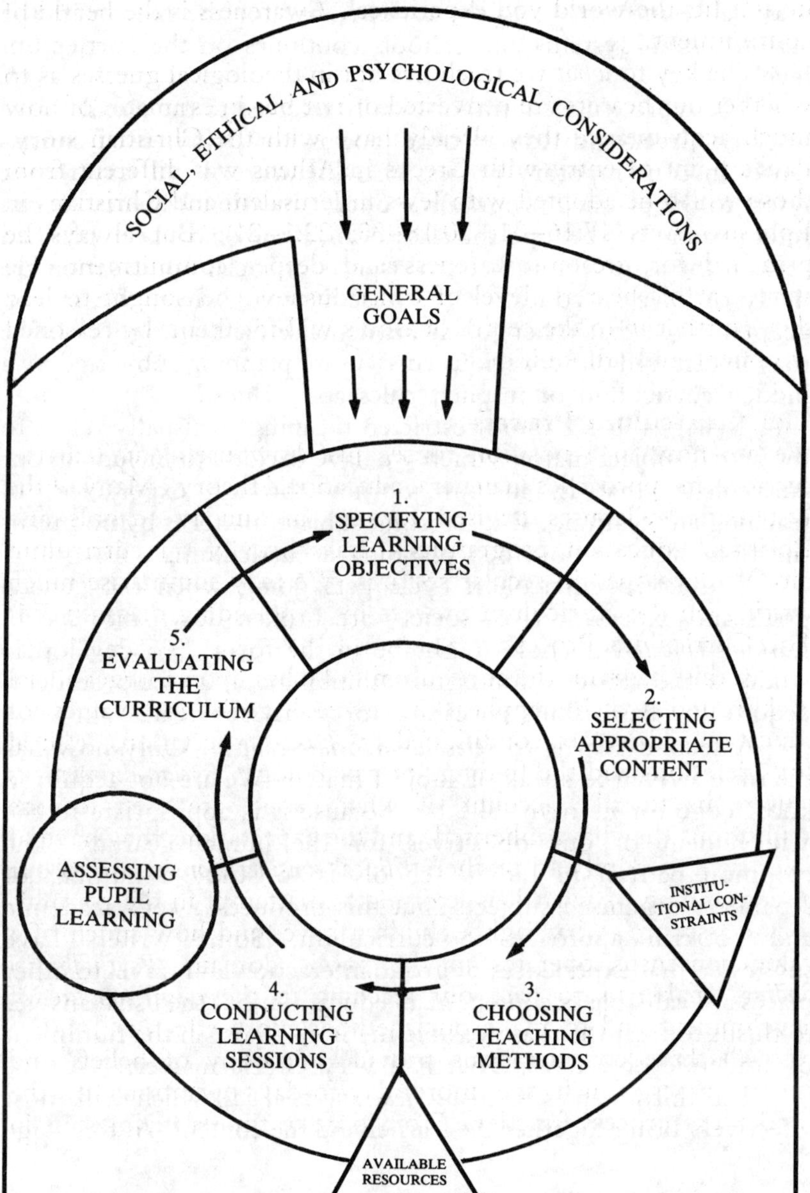

research emphasis, or a public enquiry into the goals of education, may cause movement in the canopy, but for the most part the action within systems and schools continues on the curriculum level.

The word 'curriculum' originally referred to the circular race track of Greek and Roman times and is not always used consistently in contemporary professional literature. I will say that it refers to the planned programme of an educational agency. It can refer to activities beyond the classroom, if they have been planned for, on the assumption that any aspects of social organisation are likely to have an educative (or miseducative) effect. We saw in chapter three that where such incidental effects are ignored, we may in fact find our conscious curriculum planning subverted by a hidden curriculum of implicit rules and values.

'Syllabus' has a more restricted meaning. It usually refers to the actual subject matter which we have decided to include in our curriculum, that is, in our journey through experiences of teaching and learning. But selecting subject matter is by no means the first thing to do when planning a curriculum.

The actual curriculum cycle gets going when the general goals and expectations of society are broken down into *specific learning objectives*. These might be in the form: 'To develop in students the capacity for critical thinking' or 'to help students acquire the basic skills necessary for social survival'.

A second step is to *select appropriate content*. Only now has the time arrived to speak of subject matter. We are not acquiring knowledge for its own sake but because it is appropriate to the achievement of our objectives for the human learner. The common pattern in public schools is to study a number of separately organised subjects, but this produces a very academic and bookish approach to curriculum. Some writers have suggested that experiences of group interaction and travel to other places are valuable as content in an education, but the usual answer to this is to treat them as possible methods to use in the fulfilment of academic objectives. That is a very Greek answer.

The third step is to *choose teaching methods* which will most effectively bring together the learner and the content. At this stage much help is available from psychological studies of how humans learn, what things interest them, and how our faculties develop throughout life. Practical limitations will be imposed on our creativity by budget, the premises available, and the level of training of our teachers. These are institutional constraints about which we must be realistic. On a more positive note, there are probably many available resources — books, teaching aids, curriculum kits, community resources — on which we can draw to enhance the educational experience.

Each of these steps has to do with the prior PLANNING of our teaching activities, but eventually we are ready to *conduct learning sessions*. This phrase is preferred to 'take lessons', which sounds very teacher-centred and piecemeal. The good teacher does not think in terms merely of separate 40-minute lessons, but of sequences of learning, spreading over several periods of time and embracing a variety of kinds of learning experience. This is the stage of PRESENTING.

After planning and presenting comes EVALUATING. In formal education no teacher worth his salt teaches, or guides learning, without periodically checking whether his efforts are having any effect. This presents, perhaps, a marked contrast to the average preacher of sermons! Evaluation operates at two levels. One is evaluation of pupil progress. The other is evaluation of the curriculum itself. Many teachers treat these questions as one and the same. They regard the tests they set children as doing both jobs. But, strangely, when students do poorly on tests, it is rare for teachers to interpret this as evidence either of poor curriculum design or bad teaching! The student generally takes all the blame.

Assessing pupil learning is a process intended to help the pupil, not to humiliate him or her. It can be used to diagnose and correct errors in learning, and to guide the pupil in setting future targets for learning and in choosing a career. The sad fact is that elitist influences have led to a situation in which assessment commonly brings good news to the few and bad news to the majority, leading to loss of self-esteem. Whereas it should inform pupils as to how well they have mastered what they have studied, in fact it mostly tells them how far they fall short statistically of their more able peers. Christian teachers should be active to render policies of assessment more humane and useful to the learner.

Evaluating the curriculum is a different matter, and an indispensable part of the curriculum cycle. While it is possible to look at test-results of pupil learning and discover quite a deal about how adequate and relevant our pupils have found the curriculum to be, we usually need to use other evaluation procedures as well. One is almost the reverse of pupil assessment: it is where the teacher invites the students, by discussion or by making anonymous responses to an evaluation form, to evaluate the course (and, by implication, the teacher). The course is, after all, meant to be for their benefit! Several other procedures for curriculum evaluation have also been developed.

The reason for carrying out such evaluations is not just to post-mortem the corpse of previous efforts but to modify and enliven one's future efforts. The results of an evaluation may cause us to revise a curriculum from the top down, e.g. we may even find it necessary to re-phrase our learning objectives, let alone our teaching procedures. So the cycle is renewed. Evaluation must be *continuous*, even after we think we have stabilised our content and methods at a good level, because the body of learners is ever-changing, always different. Any change in society or cultural consciousness (which will eventually filter down to re-adjustments of subject-matter) will be felt first in the way our students react to our teaching. Their perception of what is going on is vital to the continuously evaluating teacher.

Here, then, in summary, is a fairly standard view of the curriculum process as it operates in general education through schooling. Controversies bestrew the literature on the subject, the most significant being the debate between those who believe curriculum should be decided in advance and those who advocate an 'emergent curriculum' which evolves from the sensed needs of the learner at the time. There is a certain affectation in such a debate, for it is not a question of whether or not to direct the learner, but how far. The very act of establishing an educational environment (whether it is called school, resource centre or whatever) betokens that some people believe they have the right and the perception to influence what others will learn. Few theorists are bold enough to advocate total freedom for learners to react in any way they choose to the open society. No education is neutral, not even when the choice is to make no formal provision for it.

Relevance to Christian Teaching

The question we must now ask is: how relevant is this model of the curriculum process to the kinds of teaching activity we engage in within, and on behalf of, the Christian faith-community?

The first observation is that we do not rely merely on social factors and value consensus to provide us with our general goals of teaching. The Christian faith is more than a humanly devised belief system or philosophical stance. It is the result of hearing a message from God, who has broken through into our space-time continuum to reveal his good purpose, and to assure us that this good purpose will be realised despite the rebellious condition into which our species has fallen. Human speculation about the nature and destiny of persons has been overtaken by communications from the Maker. Our general goals are to draw persons to Christ and to encourage them to be his ambassadors in a multi-faith society.

We still need, as diagram 5.1 suggests, to take heed of *social* structures and expectations in setting our learning objectives. Yet not with a view to 'letting the world write the agenda for the church', but rather to discovering points of intersection with the universal gospel, so that our applications of Scripture to the challenge of developing a contemporary life-style will have prophetic relevance. *Ethical* considerations, enriched by the law of neighbour-love, will also continue to affect our curriculum development, particularly in relation to the complementary opportunities which compulsory and voluntary learning environments provide.

Psychological findings, too, will be taken into account in our choices of context, content and method, along with a much greater respect for individual needs and goals than is common in most secular educational models. It is not that non-Christian theorists don't claim to meet the needs of the individual, but they often work from inadequate views of the nature of persons and slip into either heavily deterministic models of self-hood or overly romantic views of human potential.[6] The Christian takes heed to the individual's capacity — and duty before God — to make responsible personal decisions about life, including decisions about what one needs to learn.

In seeking especially to nurture Christian youth and adults in their commitment, our Master's example compels us to establish our specific learning objectives in consultation with the prospective learners. Apart from any humanistic reasons which might be given for such a policy (as in the writings of many advocates of 'free schools'), there are further distinctively Christian grounds for it, reflected in the verse quoted from Jeremiah by the writer to the Hebrews: "No longer will a man teach his neighbour, or a man his brother, saying 'Know the Lord', because they will all know me, from the least of them to the greatest" (Heb 8:11; cf. Jer 31:34; Isa 54:13; John 6:45). I understand this passage not to be saying that Christians haven't anything to teach each other, but that the converted believer derives from his restored relationship with God a heightened perception of his own spiritual interests. The young Christian is not an ignoramus; he has often been known to teach his elders some fresh perspective on a biblical passage.

From time to time, then, a community of believers will review its knowledge of Scripture, its interactions with the wider culture, and the sensed individual needs of its members, and formulate *specific objectives* for its teaching programme. We can derive considerable value from secular models of curriculum planning at this point, not so much in the substance of our aims, as in the form in which we express them. I will return to this point in a more practical way in the next chapter.

The second stage of the classical curriculum cycle is also relevant to our purposes, for the same reason. It is the stage of selecting *appropriate content*. Naturally enough, a Christian community of believers will turn constantly to the Scriptures as source and norm of its faith. But there will also be decisions to make about where and how often to bring in study topics drawn from contemporary living in the industrial society. I will return to this point in chapter seven.

The classical curriculum strategy fails us, however, in its next move. The usual response is to move on to a consideration of teaching methods, *taking for granted* the whole edifice of schooling. Many approaches to Christian education curriculum do the same. But for all the reasons advanced in previous chapters, we must avoid any such automatic assumption.

In a curriculum model for Christian teaching, we need a step which identifies *appropriate learning environments*. This will prompt us to set our specified objectives against the kinds of learning environments found in the home, the open community, and the various types of group commonly formed within faith-communities. We will also take into account the biblical injunctions and models studied in chapter two. I will discuss these issues in more detail in chapter eight.

Now we can proceed to the next PLANNING phase, which is the choice of appropriate *teaching methods and resources*. There is a bewildering array of published materials and study resources on the Christian market. They tempt us to pick interesting material out of the catalogue or off the shelf without first thinking through the needs of one's own particular faith-community and clarifying the questions of objectives, content and learning environments. We then find ourselves enslaved by someone else's perceptions of what people need to know and how they should be taught. Particularly is this true of curriculum material produced in other countries, such as the USA and Britain. The Australian culture is sufficiently different from either to make it essential that we do our homework on the first three stages of our curriculum development *before* shopping for pre-packaged resources.

At last, as in the classical model, we are ready to *conduct our learning sessions*. And also, as in the classical model, we need to build in procedures by which we can *evaluate the curriculum*. But teaching for commitment requires us again to modify the classical model of secular educational theory. For we have seen in the early part of the present chapter that we are committed to *encourage appropriate responses*, whether of worship, repentance or public

Diagram 5.2 A CURRICULUM MODEL FOR TEACHING IN THE CHURCH

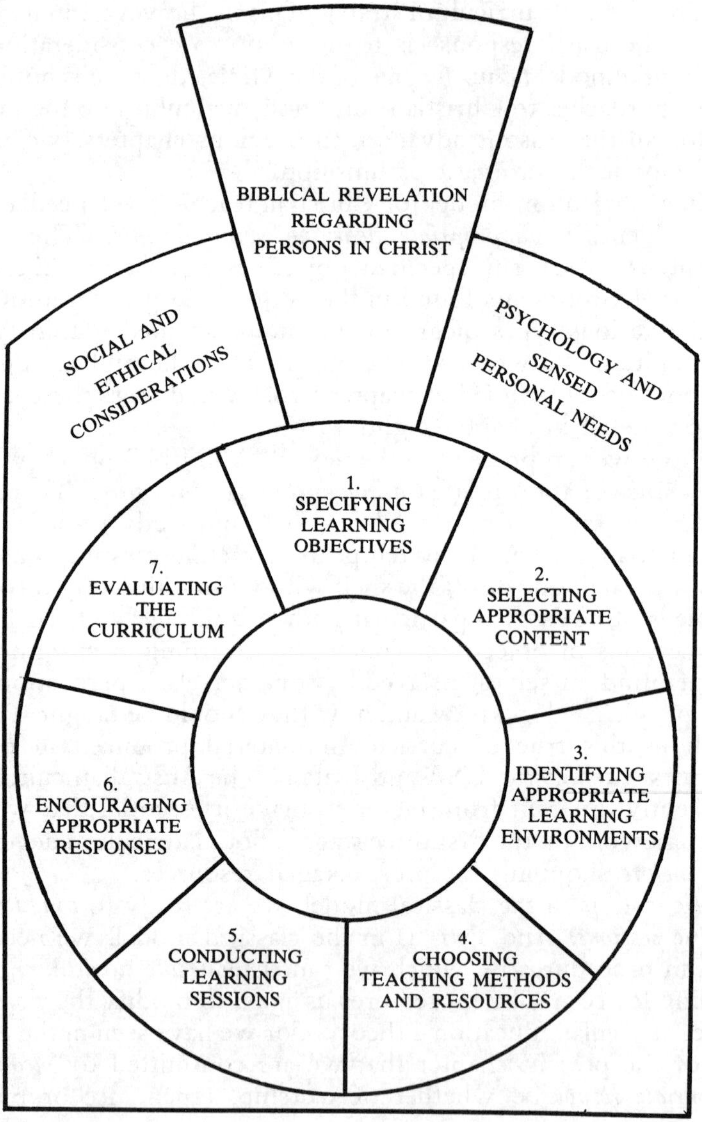

witness. We must not remain in the closed circle of self-development. What we learn should prompt us to break out in praise and loving action. When we come to evaluate the curriculum, one of our criteria of success will be whether it has borne fruits of this kind. Did it win some to initial commitment? Did it lead the committed to worship more deeply and serve more effectively? Did it draw out the gifts of teaching distributed through the body of believers? Did it develop the gifts of all for the works of service to which they have been called? Such issues will be taken up in chapter nine.

From all this there emerges a modified analysis of the curriculum cycle, hopefully more Judaeo-Christian and adapted to the strategy of teaching for commitment. I have tried to represent it in diagram 5.2. I believe it has something to offer in the wider arena of public education, but my concern here has been to demonstrate its relevance to the teaching ministries within the community of faith. In the next chapter I want to comment in more practical detail on the first stage, namely, the specification of learning objectives.

Footnotes

1. R. Trigg, *Reason and Commitment* (Cambridge: Cambridge University, 1973) 43f.
2. I do not intend by these remarks to diminish the need to pursue these theological issues further in the church, but only to say that we can get on with our essential teaching ministries without needing to suppose that the resolution will require us to alter our approach. See R. Buckland, *Children of the King* (Sydney: ANZEA, 1979) for further useful discussion of this.
3. These requirements for reasonable faith bear some resemblance to the specifications for religious education in the public school. That is why effective religious studies can, from the standpoint of the Christian faith, justifiably be viewed as *pre-evangelistic*, even though that is not its secular objective.
4. Westerhoff, *Children*, 39.
5. Some of the recognised classics are H. Taba, *Curriculum Development: Theory and Practice* (New York: Harcourt Brace and World, 1962); P.H. Hirst, *Knowledge and the Curriculum* (London: Routledge and Kegan Paul, 1975) and R.W. Tyler, *Basic Principles of Curriculum and Instruction* (Chicago: University of Chicago, 1971). Useful recent surveys include Michael Goldby, *etal.*, eds., *Curriculum Design* (London: Croom Helm, 1975) and John D. McNeil, *Curriculum* (Boston: Little, Brown and Co., 1977).
6. I have explored this issue in my *Education and the Endangered Individual* (New York: Teacher's College, 1973).

6

Specifying Learning Objectives

The time has arrived to get down to specifics. In this chapter we will discuss issues affecting our framing of learning objectives for Christian teaching ministries. The point has already been made that the first step is not to nominate the content we think people ought to study, but the objectives that we as Christian teachers have derived from considering people's needs and interests in the light of Scripture.

Our first task is to see if the Bible provides any kind of overarching general *aim*, and I will show that it does. Next, I will discuss the extent to which factors of human *development* from child to adult cause this aim to be modified for different age groups. Then we will look at the *form* in which it is most useful to express our objectives, relating this to techniques of *need-assessment* and to questions regarding the *scope* of Christian ministries. Some *examples* of objectives statements will then follow.

A General Aim

Is there a general aim to which all specific objectives must ultimately point? On Scriptural evidence the answer is an unqualified yes. There are many pointers in the Bible to the qualities to be looked for in a mature Christian. A classic passage in Ephesians chapter four gathers up many of the threads. It says that God distributes spiritual gifts amongst the believers in a faith-community, including the gift of teaching, in order

> to prepare God's people for works of service, so that the body of Christ may be built up until we all reach unity in the faith and in the knowledge of the Son of God and become mature, attaining the full measure of perfection in Christ. Then we will no longer be infants, tossed back and forth by the waves, and blown here and there by every wind of teaching and by the cunning and craftiness of men in their deceitful scheming. Instead, speaking the truth in love, we will in all things grow up into him who is the Head, that is, Christ. (Eph 4:12–15)

The notion of 'perfection in Christ' is beautifully filled out in an earlier verse of the same letter, when Paul says that 'in him you too are being built together to become a dwelling in which God lives by his Spirit.' (Eph 2:22)[1]

Descending from these heavenly harmonies to spell out the criteria of spiritual growth in more prosaic terms, we may deduce the following:

1. We aim to draw persons into faith-relationship with God in Christ.
2. Having turned to him, each person can and must seek to 'grow in him'; that is, grow more like him in mind and will, and become more sensitised to his presence within one's personality.
3. The environment within which this growth is meant to take place is the community of fellow-believers. Hence maturity is characterised as *unity* in belief, *diversity* in gifts, and *interdependence* in improving our knowledge of God and our service to other persons.
4. What we learn is meant not to remain as mere head-knowledge, but to be translated continuously into action as we speak the truth in love and perform works of service within and beyond the faith-community.

In a sentence, we are to DRAW persons to God, that they may GROW in him, maturing in COMMUNITY with other believers, issuing in SERVICE to all persons. Whatever specific objectives we formulate must be judged by these four hallmarks of Christian development.

Developmental Factors

A footnote to these remarks on content concerns the degree to which this general description is likely to vary with the stage of natural development reached by the individual. Is the description for adults only, or has it application to young children and adolescents as well? Quite apart from spiritual questions, there are physical and psychological aspects of human development which affect the individual's capacity to relate to others, to understand beliefs, and to translate beliefs into consistent loving actions.

The first answer is that if we work on the model of teaching for commitment described in the previous chapter, then we will simultaneously be encouraging both the initial turning and subsequent growing towards God, whatever the age group to which we are ministering. Rather than imposing some kind of 'K-12 curriculum' on learners, we will be adapting our teaching to that level of awareness of God which we perceive in each individual child.

Secondly, we will not hold back from the aim of drawing young children to God just because there is some evidence that they cannot handle the concept of 'God' at a high level of abstraction. While there are intellectual aspects of the faith that will boggle young minds (some of which boggle most adult minds as well!), the nub of Christianity is relationship with our heavenly Father through his Son, and the divine analogy of parenthood will develop in their minds through concrete experiences of the caring family and faith-community. Similarly, in inciting them to 'works of service', our emphasis will be upon not salvation by works but enrichment of caring relationships with others in need, again inviting comparison with the divine analogy. Concrete experiences will provide the building blocks for a fuller conceptual grasp of such basic Christian beliefs in later years.

Conversely, even when we come to consider teaching

ministries on behalf of those who are chronologically adult, we will continue to rely upon concrete experiences of relationship with God and one's fellow-believers to put flesh on the bones of doctrinal study, and we will balance such inputs with calls to service and testimony.

Hence, the general aim holds good at all developmental stages. The four hallmarks it generates are appropriate tests to be applied to any specific learning objectives we formulate, whatever the age group or target audience.

Framing Objectives Statements

We turn now to the technical question of the form in which we should express our learning objectives. This is a matter in which general theorists of curriculum can be of considerable help. There are three faulty approaches to beware of.

The first is to *ignore the need for stating objectives*. Pastor X gets the idea that it would be good for his people if he were to start a week-night Bible study group. His first disappointment is that few turn up. The second is that fewer still remain after a few weeks. Yet what could be more desirable than encouraging his people to study the Word? Aren't they, he asks himself, genuinely committed to the Lord?

It is premature to judge others in this way. People respond readily to proposed programmes which seem likely to meet specific needs. Pastor X failed to canvass the needs and interests of his people. The impression created by his announcement of the programme was that since it was a religious duty to study the Bible, people must commit themselves to a weekly engagement with no foreseeable end in order to be in good standing with the pastor (or, indeed, with God!). Lacking stated objectives, this defective motive became the implicit objective of the programme.

Had the pastor stated that he was offering, say, a course in understanding how to use and interpret the Bible; or a study of the first Letter to Timothy focusing on how to improve the connection between belief and behaviour; or an enquiry into Christian witness in the workforce, drawing on biblical resources; or some other such purposeful activity; then it is possible he would have attracted a larger and more interested group. If he still failed to do so, then it would more likely be a sign of faulty needs-assessment by him than half-hearted commitment on the part of his flock.

The second faulty approach is to *state objectives in vague and general terms.* 'To help members grow in grace', for example, is a laudable intention derived from our earlier search for an overall goal, but it doesn't give much indication of the particular learning activity to follow. More specific targets are called for if a programme is to have a sense of purpose and achievement.

The third faulty approach is to *state objectives always in terminal, behavioural form.* In reaction to the vagueness of earlier attempts to state objectives for school syllabuses and programmes, a research emphasis developed which required that our objectives translate all the desired outcomes of learning into specific observable responses or performances. 'Behavioural objectives' therefore referred to things the learner must be able to *do* at the end of an instructional sequence, e.g. 'the student must be able to name all the bones of the human skeleton (or all the kings of Israel and Judah!)'.

This approach is useful for some kinds of learning, especially at the levels of mechanical learning and skills development, e.g. the skills of finding biblical references, using a concordance, leading a business meeting, and so on. But extreme behaviourists insist that *all* objectives must be reduced to this form.[2] This obscures the validity and importance of changes in one's intellectual grasp of large areas of thought, of individual choice and creativity, enduring dispositions and long-term intentions, and of the exploration of inter-personal relationships. Strict behaviourism was a deterministic, mechanical model of persons inadequate to account for the marks of spirit in them.

A balanced approach will recognise that there are some lower-order *skills* and areas of basic *knowledge* which it is valuable for the growing Christian to acquire, and which can and ought to be identified in terminal instructional objectives-statements. There are other *capacities* and *understandings* which may need to be stated more open-endedly, as when one speaks of developing an understanding of the doctrine of justification by faith, or a capacity to counsel young people disturbed by friction or break-up in the family.

Then there are *dispositions* which we will want to encourage, such as a readiness to perform practical services for people in need, to act as peace-makers in times of interpersonal conflict, to pray first when encountering stress, to commend life in Christ when opportunity arises, to adore God when our attention is arrested by some instance of his power, creativity or love. It is helpful to view the 'fruit of the Spirit' (Gal 5:22) as Spirit-implanted, yet nurtured by Christian teaching. This will be all the more effective when dispositions are written in, where relevant, to the learning objectives of particular programmes.

Needs-Assessment

One of the tendencies in general educational theory, mostly concerned as it is with schooling, has been to stress the dominant role of the professional teacher in deciding what will be taught. Curriculum objectives are foreordained by one's theory of general education, and the needs of the learner function merely as psychological constraints on how far in practice teachers can approach their pre-set objectives. These objectives, of course, are supposed to be based on what are considered to be the learner's real needs and best interests in the long run. But the fact remains that the learner encounters them as external demands placed upon him or her.[3]

There is an analogy to this state of affairs in the faith-community also. The biblical revelation is, in the first instance, an external authority which prescribes objectives for our teaching ministries. Some churches have therefore been too easily drawn to the more authoritarian curriculum models available, prescribing tightly organised syllabuses which forbid deviation from, or questioning of, the denominational package. The Christian personality they work towards is fixed in its beliefs, dogmatic in its opinions, and narrow and conformist in its behaviour.

To repeat the findings of earlier chapters, people did not originally come to know Christ this way. Unity of faith is to be found through knowledge and enquiry; the conquest of doubt through the further exploration of Scripture and external evidences. Christ's dealings with individuals were as diverse in approach as those individuals were different from each other. He met them on their present level of awareness and spoke to their individual needs. The responses he sought from them were not religiously stereotyped but tailored to their own unique personality patterns. Nicodemus was challenged intellectually, the woman at the well in her self-image, the rich young ruler in his attitude to the poor. Jesus' disciples retained their individuality, to the church's gain, giving us four independent perspectives on the gospel story, and further illuminating the Way in the Epistles through the 'mysticism' of John, the synthesising mind of Paul, the rocky fortitude of Peter, the practicality of James, and so on. The early church was not uniformly composed either of middle-class, short-back-and-sides home-owners or unemployed young zealots. It met needs at all levels.

One secular author, Malcolm S. Knowles, whose particular concern is adult education, is so discontented with standard teacher-centred pedagogy that he has attempted to popularise a new word for the teaching process — 'andragogy'. Traditional pedagogy (Gk. *paid-agogos*: child leading) treats the learner as a dependent personality who must be directed to learn what adults think ought to be known. 'Andragogy' (Gk. *andr-*: man), says Knowles, is 'the art and science of helping adults learn',[4] and involves encouraging adults to direct their own learning and to decide for themselves what teachers and resources they wish to draw on.

Knowles recognises that a sharp contrast should not be drawn between the respective ways in which children and adults learn. He voices the suspicion that much of what he says about andragogy probably holds for the teaching of children as well, but he does not pursue this since his concern is in the area of adult education. Nevertheless, for reasons given in earlier chapters, I believe we must view Christian teaching ministries from a vantage point which places emphasis at *all* stages on participant learning. One very practical reason for doing so, incidentally, is that if we don't, working as we do for the most part in voluntary settings, our clients will vote with their feet, as in the case of Pastor X's ill-starred attempt to launch a Bible-study group.

The Bible is relevant to the learner in two ways: (a) as it awakens a sense of need and awareness of God, and (b) as it speaks to this need at various levels of personal and social existence. Hence it is not a denial of the authority of revelation to say that we should have regard to the sensed needs and interests of our people in designing our teaching programmes. The real debate about the place of the Bible in our programmes comes at the next stage, when selecting content appropriate to the objectives we have chosen.

At all age levels our choice of objectives should be influenced by what we are able to find out about the needs and interests of the learners. With small children we will probably feel that we know a lot better than they what goals to aim at, and our sampling of their attitudes will occur in the natural course of presenting our programme to them. With fellow adults the Christian teacher is on more nearly equal terms, and should be inviting them to share in the formulation (and evaluation) of programme objectives. In between these two levels there is need for an increasing measure of student participation in specifying objectives, and a careful withdrawal of teacher direction over time, much as we expect good parents to slacken and eventually relinquish the reins on their maturing children.

It can be very threatening to all concerned for a teacher to sit down with a group of older children or adults and say: 'Well, what would you like to learn?' But we should be working for the day when some church members at least will have matured in their Christian growth to the point where this is a possible and profitable approach. Steps along the way to this goal might include:

(a) Advertising a planning meeting to decide the next term's programme focus, and inviting all interested to attend, either to observe or make suggestions.
(b) Setting up a small planning group with specified learner representation on it.

(c) Using an exploratory questionnaire with a wide selection of possible themes to choose from, based on the general needs of such groups, as identified in the research literature (see examples later in the chapter).

(d) Basing a programme on several small group electives rather than one prescribed learning route for everybody.

The Scope of Our Aim

Finally, we should remind ourselves of the scope embraced by the general aim of Christian teaching ministries. Our minds run naturally to intellectual studies — biblical, theological and cultural — because we are habituated to the model of formal instruction in the literary-academic mode, for the reasons given in previous chapters. And there *is* a basic salvation-story to be learnt, understood and applied to contemporary living. It is this, as we said in chapter four, which informs our evangelistic proclamation, inspires our worship and growth in grace, and focuses our witness in society.

But we are more than merely rational minds. We have feelings towards ourselves and others. We discover new worlds of experience by entering into relationships with other persons. We are influenced far more than we know by social conditioning and sub-conscious traumas. We have attitudes and beliefs to unlearn as well as to learn, and so the objectives of Christian teaching must include reducing anxieties (Phil 4:6; Matt 6:25–27); rebuilding self-esteem in those wounded by physical exploitation, inferiority feelings, or mental deterioration[5]; helping those with physical limitations to accept themselves and feel accepted (Luke 5:12–14; 19:1–9); leading the brother or sister still addicted to legalistic regulations into liberty without depriving him or her of security (1 Cor 8:1–13); and inducing sobriety, integrity and sound speech in others by our own example (Tit 2:7–8, 15).

Intrinsic to the tasks of teaching are objectives of *training*. We are not merely co-operating in God's restoring work in the personalities of those who believe, but in his commission to them to go forth and disciple others. The point of making people 'wise for salvation' is so that they may then be 'thoroughly equipped for every good work' (2 Tim 3:15–16).[6] To this end our objectives must include the drawing out of gifts and the delegation of increasing responsibility for ministries. The true teacher and pastor are always sharing not only their message but their ministries: training their successors, equipping others to teach others also (2 Tim 2:2). This policy was splendidly exemplified in the literacy programme which grew out of Frank Laubach's well-known ministry amongst the Moro tribe in the Philippines after 1930, typified by the slogan 'Each one teach one'.[7]

Hence we are concerned with learnings of many kinds. *Learning to think* is essential but not sufficient. We also want to help believers to handle their *feelings* and develop more Christian *dispositions*. We want to strengthen *self-esteem* based on the calm assurance that our life 'is now hidden with Christ in God' (Col 3:3) and we are free at last to love our neighbours as we love our God-accepted self (Luke 10:27). We want to help believers to give themselves to caring *relationships*, to develop their *special gifts* of service and leadership, and to learn *responsibility in ministry*. These seven spheres of Christian development provide another check-list for appraising the objectives we formulate for our teaching programmes. Ours is a whole-person gospel.

In summary, there are various ways in which we may formulate objectives for organised teaching programmes. Diagram 6.1 provides a check-list of criteria by which to evaluate our formulations.

About the Examples

The examples which follow include (a) a sample questionnaire used in one church to assess adult needs and interests; (b) a needs-assessment report for youth-work developed in another church; (c) a set of objectives for a study course examining Christian education, and (d) a set of objectives for a workshop on self-esteem.

The questionnaire in our first example is a modification of two such instruments actually used by the author at various times. This fact underlines the need to respond to your own local situation, not using a questionnaire developed somewhere else or in a text-book as it stands. For instance, the questionnaire shown here may be far too detailed for the community of believers to

Diagram 6.1 A CHECK-LIST FOR
EVALUATING OBJECTIVES STATEMENTS [8]

BIBLICAL HALLMARKS:

Does this set of objectives help in some way to:

1. *Draw* persons closer to God in Christ?
2. Encourage them to *grow* more mature in faith?
3. Foster gift-development within the faith-*community*?
4. Prompt active *ministries* on behalf of others?

PSYCHO-SOCIAL FACTORS

Do these objective statements:

5. Relate clearly to the developmental stage reached by these particular learners?
6. Respond to each learner's own perceived needs?
7. Recognise the socio-economic influences which are tending to shape each learner?

SPECIFICITY

Are these objective statements:

8. Clear enough to identify what specific outcomes would count as evidence of successful teaching?
9. Limited enough to provide this particular programme with a defined purpose and end-point?

SCOPE

Does the scope of these objective statements include:

10. *Cognitive* gains in critical understanding of the faith and its applications to life in society?
11. *Affective* gains in the quality of the feelings we have towards God, ourselves, other persons and nature?
12. *Dispositional* gains (fruit of the Spirit)?
13. Gains in a Christ-based *self-esteem*?
14. Gains in the ability and desire to enter into caring *relationships*?
15. Gains in personal *gift*-development?
16. Successful assumption of *responsibility* in various spheres of leadership and ministry?

which you belong, or may reflect a different social situation from yours. Borrow ideas, by all means, but don't feel you have to adhere slavishly to another person's model. This example, however, illustrates a few principles to keep in mind.

Example 1: A SAMPLE ADULT NEEDS-ASSESSMENT QUESTIONNAIRE

WHAT I WOULD LIKE TO SEE IN
A PROGRAMME FOR OLDER YOUTH AND ADULTS

PART A

NAME .... PHONE: ....

ADDRESS .... SEX: Circle M or F

.... Postcode ....

CATEGORY (Put one of the following sets of letters in the box):

YS	= upper school student	AW	= working adult (FT or PT)
YW	= working youth under 18	AH	= home duties only
YN	= youth under 18 not presently working	AN	= adult not presently working
YT	= technical or tertiary student	AR	= retired adult

PREFERRED SPHERE OF WORK (Optional. If employed, please supply descriptive job title. If unemployed, your preference):

....

HOME SITUATION (Put one of the following in the box):

N	= no present married partner	M	= married, but no dependent children
NC	= no present partner, but with dependent children	MC	= presently married, with dependent children

PART B

Below are listed a number of ways of exercising our respective Christian gifts, for the benefit of those in the Christian community and beyond. We'd like you to help us widen the possibilities by identifying contributions you think you can make, if not straight away, at least after training. Put a cross on the appropriate line for each ministry to which you think you might be fitted.

	Available now	*Would value training*	*Available only after training*
In Community			
1. To babysit for a parent needing a break during the day.	....	....	....
2. To help care for handicapped children.	....	....	....
3. To shop for or chauffeur the housebound.	....	....	....
4. To help young children learn about the faith.	....	....	....
5. To assist in primary school religious studies.	....	....	....
6. To help with club activities for primary children.	....	....	....
7. To teach hand-crafts.	....	....	....
8. To coach sport. Which?	....	....	....
9. To do art-work and lay-out.	....	....	....
10. To assist in secondary school religious studies.	....	....	....
11. To help in youth group leadership.	....	....	....
12. To lead small Bible study groups for youth.	....	....	....
13. To help with technical equipment.	....	....	....
14. To repair and maintain furniture.	....	....	....
15. To garden for those in special need.	....	....	....
16. To cook for those in special need.	....	....	....
17. To mend clothing for those in special need.	....	....	....
18. To clean house for those in special need.	....	....	....
19. To visit the sick.	....	....	....
20. To counsel people with problems in the home.	....	....	....

	Available now	*Would value training*	*Available only after training*
21. To counsel troubled marriage-partners.	....	....	....
22. To counsel sufferers from pain or grief.	....	....	....
23. To do office-work and typing.	....	....	....
24. To pastor a family worship cluster.	....	....	....
25. To exercise skills of Christian writing.	....	....	....
26. To help in financial accounting.	....	....	....
27. To lead small Bible study groups for adults.	....	....	....
28. To help aged persons in practical ways.	....	....	....
29. To be a confidential telephone listener.	....	....	....
30. To translate for migrants — (Languages ....)	....	....	....
31. Other	....	....	....
In large-group worship			
32. To prepare prayers and lead in prayer.	....	....	....
33. To read the Bible passage.	....	....	....
34. To welcome and host newcomers.	....	....	....
35. To plan and lead the overall service.	....	....	....
36. To preach.	....	....	....
37. To help with the music. If so, how?	....	....	....
38. Other?	....	....	....

Now would you look back over the items in Part B which you marked with an 'x', and identify say 3 or 4 which represent the ones you'd most like to be involved in. Put a ring around those x's.

(You may prefer to detach the next part and submit it anonymously)

PART C

Below are listed a number of areas likely to be of concern to the Christian who is striving to grow in life and witness. Please put crosses next to those you would value help with.

UNDERSTANDING MY FAITH

The Bible

1. How far is the Bible to be viewed as the Word of God? ......
2. An overview of the Bible. ......
3. How to interpret the Bible. ......
4. How to introduce others to the Bible. ......
5. Study of a biblical book. ......
6. Other? ....

Our God

1. How important is it to believe in the Trinity? ......
2. How much control does God exercise over the world? ......
3. How to reconcile suffering with a loving God? ......
4. Did Jesus have to die the way he did? ......
5. How could Jesus be both God and man? ......
6. How does belief in the Holy Spirit make any difference? ......
7. Other? ....

The Church, Past and Present

1. Why go to church? ......
2. Which churches are right? ......

LIVING FOR GOD

Personal

1. How to pray. ......
2. How to profit from personal Bible study. ......
3. How to worship God. ......
4. How to get guidance from God. ......
5. How to love myself. ......
6. How to overcome feelings of inferiority ......
   anxiety ......
   grief ......
   resentment ......
   loneliness ......
7. How to organise my personal time schedule. ......
8. How to cope with affluence. ......
9. How to cope with poverty. ......
10. Other? ....

Relationships

1. Sexual adjustment before marriage. ......
2. Sexual adjustment during marriage. ......
3. Adjustment after loss of a marriage partner. ......
4. Reconciling home duties, study and/or career. ......
5. Christian parenting. ......

3. Where did denominations come from? ......
4. How important are the sacraments? ......
5. What should be the roles of clergy and laity? ......
6. Understanding the cults. ......
7. Understanding other religions. ......
8. Other? ....

Our Task

1. What does evangelism involve? ......
2. What priority should we give to social action and reform? ......
3. Is 'the missionary' still needed? ......
4. Should we run church schools? ......
5. Should we sponsor church hospitals, homes, etc. ......
6. Should Christians be involved in politics? ......
7. Other? ....

6. Caring for the handicapped child. ......
7. Relating to other Christians. ......
8. Relating to non-Christians. ......
9. Relating to employers and bosses. ......
10. Other? ....

Vocation and Recreation

1. Choosing a career. ......
2. Coping with unemployment. ......
3. Balancing work, study, recreation and service. ......
4. Ambition. ......
5. Witnessing in my work-place. ......
6. Christians, unionism and industrial action. ......
7. Can a Christian have fun? ......
8. What value should we place on the arts? ......
9. Other? ....

Other Suggestions

....

....

Once again, would you look back over the items in Part C which you marked with an 'x', and identify say 7 or 8 which represent the topics of most interest to you. Put a ring around those x's.

Thank you for spending the time on this.
We'll tell you what we've learnt from the survey as soon as we can.

First, *it tries not to invade people's privacy*. It invites their participation but emphasises that they are free not to respond, if that is their wish, or to respond anonymously, at points where some might feel they were being asked to expose their inner selves. It doesn't ask for people to give their ages but makes it possible to infer general age groups from the 'Category' section. It doesn't probe for distinctions between 'single', 'separated', 'divorced' and 'widowed' which might embarrass and don't greatly matter for the purpose in hand. Enough can be learned from use of the terms: no married partner/married/dependent children.

Secondly, *it combines closed and open-ended responses*. If there were no spaces to record additional ideas or suggestions, the biggest needs might get overlooked because the questionnaire compiler didn't think of them. If there were no specific topic suggestions to be marked with an 'x', respondents might not be able to think of their own, or might, in what they did suggest, overlook major areas of Christian growth.

Thirdly, *it links ministering with learning*. I will say more about Part B in later chapters, when we explore the development of gifts, but it earned inclusion in this questionnaire so that the impression would not be given of offering learning experiences for their own sake. Learning and serving go hand in hand.

Fourthly, *it provides a range of possible study topics which makes some effort to minister to the whole person*. The intellectual is balanced with affective and relational learning, doctrine with conduct, personal needs with social responsibilities. From this needs-assessment one would then move on to frame learning objectives reflecting the major emphases which had emerged.

Example 2 contains the first report of an enquiry into youth needs which was conducted in a suburban church several years ago. The author was one of those involved. The report is reproduced largely as it then appeared, in order to provide an example with several imperfections which those who have read the chapter up to this point will be able to detect. Before reading on, subject it to critique.

Example 2: REPORT OF A YOUTH NEEDS ENQUIRY

As a result of (a) evidence collected by questionnaire from leaders, young people, and parents; and (b) talks on Christian objectives for youth development, the Education Commission of Church X offers the following formulation of objectives for our youth programme for further discussion.

RECOGNISING that youth are whole persons with many needs, and that some of these needs are provided for, to some degree, in the wider community, we see our church's special responsibilities as being:

1. *To win youth to Christ*

   Young people vary widely in their readiness to respond to the call of Christ, but, in general, early teens need to enter into the basic personal commitment, and older teens to apply this commitment to all areas of life.

2. *To assist their Christian growth*

   This aim includes efforts to:
   (a) increase their understanding and use of the Bible;
   (b) promote personal and group prayer habits;
   (c) deepen the meaningfulness of their church worship;
   (d) nurture a sense of Christian stewardship;
   (e) encourage their moral stand in the community;
   (f) prompt them to testify personally about Christ;
   (g) fulfil the other aims listed below.

3. *To guide personality development*

   This aim relates to such aspects of development as:
   (a) *Physical* — Facilities for teenagers in this respect seem good in the community at large, and require no particular church provision.
   (b) *Mental* — Education at school caters widely for this aspect of development. However the church needs to present the Christian faith as calling us to strenuous thinking about both doctrine and behaviour. We have neglected this in our youth work.
   (c) *Socio-emotional* — Personality develops in a social context, and we believe that the larger community falls short in provision at this level. We believe that our church must provide opportunities for social life in the peer group, with older leaders functioning as advisers rather than programme organisers. Increasing participation in running their own affairs prepares teenagers for adult membership of church and society.

4. *To promote Christian social relationships*

We must create a social climate in which there is provision for:

(a) democratic participation;
(b) freedom to express one's own ideas;
(c) development of group loyalties and a sense of belonging;
(d) opportunities for personal counselling;
(e) learning to live with each other's differences of personality, ability and background;
(f) sex education;
(g) the special level of sharing unique to Christian fellowship.

5. *To provide avenues for Christian service*

This aim opens up the possibilities for service in and amongst:

(a) my home;
(b) my classmates and peers;
(c) my local church;
(d) my local community;
(e) the wider church (other denominations, mission field);
(f) the wider society.

6. *To develop Christian leadership capacities*

This aim includes the provision of opportunities to:

(a) accept increasing responsibility, in proportion to response and capacity;
(b) utilise all leadership qualities, not only intellectual;
(c) involve older adolescents in the government of the church.

It is, of course, more than a needs and objectives statement. It also begins to suggest the kinds of learning environment called for, and in this regard fails to clarify the relationship between home and church. There is, however, some attempt to anchor the identification of objectives to be met by the church in a hard-nosed appreciation of what the community at large already offers.

The first aim, referring to winning youth to Christ, is somewhat simplistic, having regard to the complexities in the notion of commitment pointed out in chapter five. The objectives associated with personality development tend to sit loose to the other, more explicitly Christian, objectives, and need to be more effectively integrated into a view of the total Christian personality.

Your critique will no doubt add to the points I have raised. The important thing is that this report was produced by a church in the midst of life, and meant a lot to those who produced it. Such an experience is in the end worth all the confident prescriptions of manuals and general research reports. Those involved then went on with a sense of direction and participation to revise their programme.

So far, my examples have referred to appraisals at the broadest programme level, producing what we may term *programme objectives*. These in turn need to be stepped down to the level of the actual courses and activities we decide to organise as a result of our needs assessments. We can refer to objectives at this level as *course objectives* or *activity objectives*.

Example 3 was taken from the actual objectives statement of the course which originally triggered the writing of the present book. The author was asked to design and teach the first of two courses in Christian education in a programme of training for the ordained ministry. These objectives resulted. Again you are invited to evaluate the set of course objectives in the light of the criteria set forward in this chapter.

Example 3: OBJECTIVES OF A CHRISTIAN EDUCATION COURSE

By the end of this unit it is expected that students will:

1. Understand the way in which current conceptions of Christian education have evolved since biblical times.
2. Be able to engage in critical analysis of current principles and policies in Christian education in the church.
3. Be disposed to conceptualise teaching in the church in a biblical rather than a secular/professional perspective.
4. Be better able to guide and co-ordinate the teaching activities within a local congregation or Christian group.
5. Be disposed to bring out the gifts of all church members and provide opportunities for their training and exercise, in preference to performing a solo part in teaching and church leadership.

It will be immediately apparent that one course can't do everything, and must be seen as contributory to a larger range of experiences together adding up to the learning programme required by a particular group. Even so, the set of objectives which I originally produced for the purpose is very cerebral, and does not give clear evidence of an intention to draw the students closer to God or to enhance their Christ-based self-esteem. These intentions may have been salvaged by the manner in which the course was actually presented, but in that case they should have been identified as objectives, not left to function as a hidden curriculum! The objectives also project an aura of schooled learning, with its requirement of pupil assessment, which was one of the constraints of the context in which it was offered.

Example 4 is of a set of objectives which was designed to set goals for a two-day workshop on the enhancement of the self-esteem of each participant. As suggested by the objectives, the programme was to include some teaching input on Scriptural perspectives (implicit in objectives 1 and 5); opportunities for assisted worship (objective 2), discussion and possibly inter-personal sensitivity training (objectives 3 and 4); and a challenge to deeper commitment (especially objective 5).

Again, one learning activity can't do everything, and this activity was apparently lacking in any explicit intention to look

Example 4: OBJECTIVES FOR A SELF-ESTEEM WORKSHOP

To help participants to:

1. Understand the source of Christian self-esteem in our acceptance by God through Christ;
2. Experience that acceptance in worship of their forgiving, renewing Lord;
3. Explore their own feelings of self-worth and inferiority in an environment of non-judgmental Christian fellowship;
4. Experience confirmation of each other in activities invoking trust, loving contact, and openness;
5. Develop the disposition to build one's interpretation of experiences, good and bad, on a positive, Christ-centred self-concept.

outward in ministry to others. This can sometimes be a serious lack in self-adjustment therapies. However, it can reasonably be assumed that within the short time available (for such adjustments take time) it was considered most wise to concentrate on a limited set of objectives, given that the participants could be expected to meet other objectives through the on-going teaching ministries of the churches to which they would probably return.

Nevertheless our check-list (diagram 6.1) prompts another criticism which is not so easily dismissed. There appeared to be no intention in this workshop to point to the development of one's spiritual gifts within the body of Christ as an activity both self-affirming and to some extent self-denying, which is intended by God to contribute to a healthy self-concept.

Footnotes

1. See also Rom 12:1–5 and 1 Cor 6:19–20. The word 'perfection' is *plērōmatos*, which conveys the idea of 'fullness' and invites the astonishing comparison with the use of the same word in Col 2:9 to describe Christ's degree of participation in the Godhead. Indeed the next verse there says: 'You have this fullness'.
2. E.g. R.F. Mager, *Preparing Instructional Objectives* (Belmont: Fearon, 1962) 12.
3. This statement is meant to identify main trends in curriculum theory. It is also true that there are dissident voices calling for learner-determined curriculum, but they have an uphill struggle against competitive employment pressures in both developed and developing nations.
4. M.S. Knowles, *The Modern Practice of Adult Education* (New York: Association, 1970) 38.
5. E.g. John 4:1–42; Acts 16:16–18; Mark 5:25–34; Luke 8:26–39. A perceptive discussion of how parents and teachers can help build and rebuild self-esteem in victims of our heartlessly competitive society is J. Dobson, *Hide or Seek* (Old Tappan: Fleming, 1974).
6. The same verb root appears in Eph 4:12, previously quoted, in the word translated 'prepare' ('prepare God's people for works of service').
7. There are interesting echoes of this objective in P. Friere's approach to adult literacy in Brazil during the sixties, described in *Pedagogy of the Oppressed* (trans. M.B. Ramos; London: Herder and Herder, 1970).
8. A useful survey of issues at a more theoretical level is volume 9, number 1 of *JCE* devoted to educational aims. There is an exciting meeting of biblical theology and educational aims in W.E. Andersen's three articles on 'The Christian Conception of Maturity' in *JCE* 3 (1960) 142–52, 4 (1961) 37–47 and 94–104.

7

Content: Bible and Life

Not until the advent of child-centred theories of education was the basic premise questioned: that the appropriate content for the church's teaching of the faithful is doctrinal belief and moral command. The source of both components was understood to be the Bible, studied directly by the Protestant, or through the filter of church decree and tradition by the average Catholic believer. In the present century much has changed. The reasons are complex.

Changing Subject Matter

We may begin to unravel the tangled skein of causation in this matter by recalling the massive social changes which occurred at the onset of the industrial revolution. The comfortable certainties of stable village and town life were swept away by new forms of work and residence. The materialistic outlook encouraged by technology and consumerism appeared to push religious concerns to the sidelines, even while the pressures of the open mass society were generating novel anxieties and ailments in the population. Those who still treasured the religious dimension felt an increasing need to make the gospel relevant to the novel variables and tensions of modern living. To put this another way, whereas the objective of Christian teaching had formerly seemed to be something one could take for granted in more stable social conditions with well-defined roles and customs, now re-definitions were needed. And it was not immediately obvious that the biblical heritage could by itself supply or service them.

Two other developments reinforced the mood of re-appraisal. One was the emergence of the new science of educational psychology, based in part on the child-centred pedagogies of such precursors as Rousseau, Froebel, Pestalozzi and Montessori. The message of the 'new education' of the 1890's was that we must cease treating children like miniature adults and help them to enjoy their present stage of life for its own sake. Content drawn from the cultural heritage should not be taught as an end in itself but as a resource to be called on if and when it was useful in coping with present experience. By analogy, religious educators were moved to question the primacy of biblical content and to recommend more attention to life experiences as content.

The second development was a challenge to the traditional view of biblical authority, making it easier to subordinate biblical knowledge to other educational priorities. This came about through the impact of 'higher criticism', an amalgam of methodologies which initially cast considerable doubt on the reliability of the biblical report. So many qualifications and cautions had to be inserted between the reader and the apparently plain meaning of Scripture that, in a manner reminiscent of the influence of the Catholic Fathers, the findings of church scholars intervened to cast the believer back on the authority of the church — derived in this case from the fluctuating claims of 'critical' scholarship.

Thus the stage was set for new approaches not only in the method but also in the content of Christian teaching ministries. But there is often a formidable cultural lag in the churches' responses to intellectual and social changes. The 'new education' came slowly to affect syllabuses of religious instruction in many American churches through the activities of the Religious Education Association referred to in chapter three. It found greatest acceptance amongst those who had also embraced the theological liberalism of the time, and it mirrored the 'activity movement' which was strongest in general education prior to the Second World War.

Similar effects were less noticeable in England until the post-war period. Then a flurry of studies showing how great were the misconceptions generated in the minds of children and youth by traditional Bible-centred methods of instruction[1] prompted experiments with 'life experience themes'. Such a suggestion was made by Ronald Goldman in *Readiness for Religion: A Basis for Developmental Religious Education*,[2] and was taken up enthusiastically by a number of educators in the sixties.

The argument was that by taking themes from the everyday experiences of children and exploring them at depth, one would *implicitly* bring into play the religious dimension of existence. Goldman sought to show how one could draw on biblical materials and incidents to assist in this depth exploration, thus presumably baptizing it into Christian nurture. It is highly significant, however, that his order of priorities required that 'life is not used to illustrate Bible truths, but the Bible is used to illustrate life's experience.'[3] As a strategy for Christian nurture it was bleached of the Christian distinctives. But in fairness it should be noted that its primary sphere of application was intended to be in religious education in the government school. As such, it was an apparently less dogmatic strategy than those currently in use, designed nevertheless to reinforce Christianity's influence in the classroom.

It is significant that one British observer, speaking in this period of the 'revolution in religious education' in which Goldman was giving a lead, chose to speak of a *twofold* revolution: a revolution in our understanding of how children think and learn, and a revolution in our understanding of what the Bible is saying.[4] To illustrate the second, theological, revolution, he referred to such books as *Honest to God* by John Robinson and *Jesus Christ and Mythology* by Rudolph Bultmann. Once again, therefore, we see a correlation between displacement of biblical content for pedagogical reasons, and displacement of its regulatory authority for theological reasons.

Does this mean that teachers and congregations whose approach to biblical interpretation is more submissive to the Bible's own authority claims are likely to be resistant to the pedagogic revolution we have just been describing? On available evidence, the answer tends to be yes. Theologically conservative churches tend to promote more Bible-centred curricula, sometimes using teaching methods not far removed from the mechanical recitation and memory work which characterised such teaching before this century.

It is not a logical necessity that they should do so. It is possible to decide that our content will be Bible-centred, but that our teaching will take account of children's needs and interests in the selection of suitable passages and teaching methods. In a book written some years ago,[5] I drew attention to an earlier revolution in the Christian teaching of school children which occurred in the nineteenth century. This revolution has been overlooked in historical surveys because it occurred for the most part outside the institution of formal schooling (whether in the church or the community at large).

It was not so much a result of the rise of Sunday schools as of widely influential groups interested in child evangelism in voluntary settings, such as the Children's Special Service Mission in Britain. Using methods which broke away from rote learning and moralistic preaching, the C.S.S.M. sought instead to present biblical material through simple questions, stories, songs and other activity methods. In a day when staid 'uniform lessons' dominated Sunday schools, and experimentally controlled studies of children's learning patterns had yet to be made, children's workers often seemed to grasp intuitively many of the principles involved. It is interesting to speculate whether, because they were working in voluntary rather than compulsory contexts, they were more sensitive to learner needs and responses.

The C.S.S.M. continues today to have striking success in its children's missions (now striving more deliberately to make contact with children in families rather than in isolation).[6] Potentially there is a reservoir here of field data which tends to be overlooked by research workers who, in the main, have studied children in the setting of formal instruction. As for the workers themselves, since it is seeing results for their efforts which keeps them going, there is a tendency to overlook the value of more systematic evaluation. The same may be said for the Inter School Christian Fellowship, a branch of the same movement working in primary and high schools in several countries. In a study of its voluntary evangelical ethos in his larger enquiry into religious education in schools, Graham Rossiter identifies the I.S.C.F. as the largest voluntary youth work in the Australian school culture.[7] But systematic empirical studies of such ministries are lacking.

Ultimately the question of what place the Bible should occupy in a programme of Christian nurture is not answerable solely on the basis of psychological studies of child development and sensed needs. Decisions about objectives and appropriate content involve value-judgments as well as factual considerations. The range of possibilities is extended by differences in theological position. An interesting illustration of this is a sample content-analysis which was undertaken by Northa Burnett of three curricula widely used in Australian churches in the seventies.[8] The analysis showed that curriculum A, serving several theologically pluralist denominations, was child-centred in method and society-oriented in content; curriculum B, an evangelical British resource also popular in Australia, was child-centred in method but Bible-centred in content; and curriculum C, an evangelical American set of publications, was Bible-centred in both content and method.[9]

Clearly, a church's choice of A, B or C would depend not only on the level of its awareness of the developmental needs of its children, but on its theological consensus vis-a-vis the authority and reliability of Scripture. It is necessary at this point for me to take a position regarding the status of Scripture in our teaching ministries, so that the deductions to follow, as we move through the curriculum cycle, will be something more than bland generalisations for all seasons.

I understand the central claim of Christianity to be the assertion that the Almighty Creator has elected to communicate intelligibly with my species. I believe him to have taken steps to ensure reliable reception and transmission of this communication: first through the spoken words of inspired seers in the OT and Jesus and the apostles in the NT; and secondly through the written record of what they said and did which we have in the

Bible. Recognising that there are some mysterious and troublesome passages in this record, and that disputes arise over the accuracy in detail of some passages, I nevertheless affirm the clarity and plain sense of the central ideas and events which convey God's proclamation to humans. And I commend the proposition that the plain message of the Bible provides the primary norm or yardstick for faith and conduct. I would expect agreement with this proposition not only amongst people who happen, like me, to be of evangelical persuasion, but amongst friends of many other theological persuasions as well.

On this understanding, foreshadowed in chapter five and presupposed in chapter six, I base the curriculum theory being developed here. For example, the general aim in the previous chapter was chosen as being both *from* Scripture and usefully representative *of* Scripture. In the next chapter, I will urge that our view of appropriate learning environments be determined by biblical precedents, rather than by taking its cue from attitudes in the general culture. And in chapter nine I will advocate views of leadership and teacher identification which derive from my reading of NT patterns. In such ways, I am striving to make biblical revelation the keystone of my curriculum perspective, as it was represented in diagram 5.2.

States of Mind in Bible Readers

Given the unique status of the Bible as inspired revelation, it is to be expected that people will approach it with a variety of states of mind, ranging from superstitious awe to scepticism. It is helpful to categorise possible mental sets, in order to anticipate what should be our teaching strategy in particular cases. I propose to discuss six possibilities, drawing out the implications of each for teaching the Bible. They are shown in diagram 7.1.

The *magical* attitude is exhibited in the kind of evangelism, referred to in chapters four and five, which fires biblical terms at people until their incomprehension magically switches to comprehension, disdaining to translate or look for middle-ground concepts which relate biblical truth to contemporary experience. It is also exhibited in the mechanical approach to guidance which

Diagram 7.1 POSSIBLE STATES OF MIND WHEN APPROACHING THE BIBLE

1. *magical*	The primary motive is the need for security, shown in a readiness to attribute superstitious powers to the recitation of proof texts arbitrarily selected.
2. *devotional*	The primary motive is communion, built on the belief that the Bible speaks for, and of, the one true God, and carries conviction, correction and encouragement from him.
3. *analytical*	The primary motive is critical-analytic study, working from the presupposition that the Bible's claim to mirror God's word is validated by the inspired full reliability of the record.
4. *neutral*	The primary motive is curiosity, fuelled by a willingness to set aside sceptical questions and encounter the documents with a temporarily open mind.
5. *sceptical*	The primary motive is critical-analytic study working from the presupposition that the Bible is a repository of fallible human speculation.
6. *hostile*	The primary motive is destructive criticism of the Bible based on opposition to the belief that God has revealed himself in Jesus.

relies on spot sampling rather than constant study. The Christian teacher needs to correct this attitude by showing how much the Bible insists on comprehension and explanation both in evangelism and in nurture.

The *hostile* attitude is a committed prejudice in the opposite direction. Making the good news known to a person in this mental state requires a lot of preliminary conversation about that person's own presuppositions and commitments; shaking the foundations, as it were, in order to invite a re-examination of the Christian option. It is in this domain that Christian apologetics — the rational defence of the Christian world-view — does its main work. It is not to be despised. Often the antagonism of the infidel is due not only to his own stubbornness but to the defective life-style of professed Christians or to encounter with the irrationalism of people with a magical view of the Bible. The Christian teacher may well rejoice at the reasonableness of the faith as he performs the teaching function of apologetic. One is reminded of Francis Schaeffer's involuntary exclamation to his wife after a night of discussion with thoughtful enquirers:

> 'It really *is* the answer, Edith; it fits, it really fits. It really *is* truth, and because it is true it fits what is really there.'[10]

The *neutral* attitude is encountered in many people who have not previously given much thought to the Bible's claims. They come to it with a temporarily open mind, willing to take it as it comes. Unaware as yet of the issues surrounding the questions of authority and inspiration, they encounter it as literature and as the archives of two belief-communities. There is no shame or waste of time in presenting it at this level. It is a stance appropriate for religious education in the classroom. The good teacher is one who can allow exploratory enquiry and doubt, in the meantime letting the Bible speak for itself. If it really is the revealed word of God, then there will be no need for a hectoring insistence that it be treated like no other book. This only has the effect of goading people to dismiss it without taking it seriously. Neutral examination of the biblical documents is pre-evangelistic in the sense that it allows the book to speak for itself, and the stories of people drawn to God through such an activity, often without Christians on hand to gild the lily, are legion.[11]

The *sceptical* attitude, as I am using the term here, represents the individual's entry into academic study of the Bible. Attempting to be objective and impartial the scholar resolves to treat the Bible as any other human book, assuming the usual amount of fallible reporting and speculative thought. Actually, it is not that simple. Documentary scholarship, even more than other kinds of scholarship, is governed by presuppositions which determine in advance the direction the enquiry will take.[12]

The great divide between liberal and evangelical scholarship comes at the point where the scholar allows more authority to the ruling model of secular enquiry than to the Bible's own claims for itself. Since neither brand of scholar is without presuppositions, it behoves the Christian teacher to be very clear on his or her own beliefs about the extent to which documents purporting to represent the word of God have been allowed by God to transmit error. The debate about inerrancy is strangely displaced, since the vital prior question is whether we grant that God is a communicating God, in *any* tangible sense. Once people are led to the conclusion that he is — by the study of, say, the fact of Christ, then their attitude to the question of biblical authority changes markedly.

There is a mediating position in this controversy, represented by the neo-orthodox stance that the Bible, though a fallible document, 'becomes the word of God' when studied by the believer in a devotional frame of mind.[13] This has some affinity with the magical approach to the Bible. It also leaves the door open for critical scholarship to do what it wishes with the extant documents, while claiming personal illumination through them from the Christ of faith. The view has had two unfortunate consequences. First, descriptions of what lies at the intelligible heart of this faith can vary from a credo indistinguishable from evangelical affirmations to one little different from benevolent humanism. Secondly, sceptical scholarship, animated by the academic demand for originality in research, can follow its model to highly eccentric conclusions which erode central truths such as the historicity of the resurrection.

The *analytical* attitude, as I am using the term here, also accepts the value of the academic approach to Bible study. Indeed it welcomes it, understanding that we are constantly admonished to strive for greater awareness and discernment, to be capable of 'correctly [handling] the word of truth' (2 Tim 2:15). Its point of entry, however, is from the prior belief that God, as part of his will to communicate authentically and intelligibly with humans, has safeguarded the record from faulty transmission. Intellectual honesty forbids that we gloss over difficulties and apparent discrepancies, but our manner of dealing with them will reflect this starting point, not the critical starting point. It is the study attitude of the person who has on other grounds — some of which may include a conviction of God's presence initially generated while reading the Bible in a more neutral frame of mind — come to 'believe that [God] exists and that he rewards those who earnestly seek him' (Heb 11:6).

An analytical approach accepts that revelation is a reliable given. The student's task is to strive for fuller understanding of what is actually revealed, having regard to its literary form and original cultural context. What, first of all, did it mean to those who first heard or read it? Then, secondly, how do these meanings transpose to my personal and cultural situation now? And thirdly, what application do they have to my present faith and conduct? I will return to these questions below in a brief excursus on *hermeneutics*.

The *devotional* attitude proceeds from the same presupposition as the analytical, but represents a more deliberately subjective and receptive mode of address. The believer subordinates intellectual curiosity for the time being in order to meditate worshipfully on God using helpful Scripture passages to do so. This is not an appeal to magic or irrationalism, since a necessary pre-requisite is that the reader have an adequate understanding of the passage being addressed. But the motive goes beyond understanding to renewal of commitment.

The Christian teacher can reasonably press learners to adopt an analytical approach to Scripture for the purpose of achieving certain specified learning objectives. But he can only teach *about* the devotional use. Even if he demonstrates the devotional use in a group act of worship, that will provide no guarantee that observing learners will enter the same mode. Indeed, to insist that they join in certain worship acts and prayers of commitment without any choice in the matter would be folly in a voluntary context and shame in a compulsory context. This is why compulsory chapel in church schools and worship assemblies in state schools and classes are violations of integrity likely to have the opposite effect from what was intended.[14]

Summary

The Christian teacher needs to be sensitive to the mental attitude with which his or her students come to the reading of the Bible. Non-believers, especially children, may be neutrally curious. In settings of compulsory instruction, direct factual encounter with the documents and the story they tell is what is called for. Some non-believers will be hostile for various reasons based on past experience. Dialogue and apologetic will be our approach with them, preparing the way for direct encounter with the Scriptures in a more open frame of mind. In both cases, we will hope to lead on to a more analytical study of the Bible, as the conviction that it is God's communication grows on the enquirer.

Such teaching activities grade into the services we want to offer to believers. Some believers have embraced faith largely on second-hand report, through preachers or media presentations. Their response to God may still be largely emotional and uninformed. We will want to bring them into direct encounter with the text, and eventually into systematic study of the full sweep of the revelation. We will also be encouraging them to build their devotional lives upon meditation of the Word.

The analytical and devotional approaches to Scripture are not mutually exclusive. In the midst of an objective analysis of a passage in its context, we may be struck by a sign of God's greatness that provokes us to pause and praise him. In the midst of a devotional meditation we may be piqued intellectually by some question raised by the passage which we resolve to follow up later. But in general it is unwise to let the one approach to the Bible do double duty. We should counsel each other to have separate times for private devotions and systematic study. Each will gain from the other, but they are different mental sets.

Excursus on Hermeneutics

Questions of historical and cultural context in relation to author and audience (both original and present) are the backbone of what has traditionally been called *hermeneutics*, or the process of interpretation. René Padilla has helpfully distinguished three approaches which may be adopted.[15]

The *intuitive* approach, as he calls it, appears in many older commentaries and much modern devotional literature. It assumes that the situation of contemporary readers (including their forms of thought and language) largely coincides with the situation represented by the original text. It is therefore appropriate to apply the word literally to one's immediate personal life. There are many points at which this direct approach works because the basic relationships between God and persons do not change their character. But as we move out to relations with other people and the larger society, it is not long before cultural differences intervene between biblical patterns of life and ours, and we are obliged to consider what certain biblical practices meant in their original context.

This leads into what Padilla calls the *scientific* approach, which seeks through the use of historical and language studies to understand what the text would have meant to the original participants and readers. A moment's reflection should be all that is needed to convince the most earnest of daily readers of the Bible (amongst whom I would like to be numbered) how much they owe to scholars in these fields. Our modern translations are the clearer and more accurate for their work. Many obscure passages have become meaningful, and all good preachers draw from the commentaries to illustrate customs that were being referred to or ideas that were being debated in particular passages. The trap is to suppose that clarifying the original meaning will necessarily reveal how it applies today, or even that the interpreters can be wholly objective in describing that meaning.

So Padilla calls for a *contextual* approach. In this, he says, 'both the context of the ancient text and the context of the modern reader are given due weight.'[16] The second of these factors reminds us that we turn to the Bible with our own needs and ways of seeing things. 'No culture as a whole reflects the purpose of God; in all cultures there are elements which conspire against the understanding of God's Word.' So western theology, says Padilla, speaking from a South American vantage point, has been affected by a materialistic and mechanistic world view. Conversely, many theologians in his own culture are translating the Gospel into an imperative of purely national or proletarian liberation. And so on. The safeguard is to keep coming back to the meaning of the Gospel in its original cultural setting, translating it into our own, and then checking back to see that we haven't lost any essential implications in the process. This is an interactive process of dialogue between Bible and modern culture which Padilla calls the 'hermeneutical circle'.[17]

Adapting Padilla, I have tried to represent the interplay in diagram 7.2. It show four stages in the process of interpretation, and the help various academic disciplines, can give to our understanding of the Word.

Groups meeting for Bible study will gain a good deal of immediate help from the clearer biblical passages, dealing with our closest relationships with God and other persons (represented as communication line AD). Luther knew that to put the Bible in the hands of the ordinary ploughman would have valid life-changing effects. But the Christian who seeks to go on to maturity and to be an effective witness in this time and place needs to complement direct word-study with studies which improve our

Diagram 7.2 STAGES IN INTERPRETING THE BIBLE

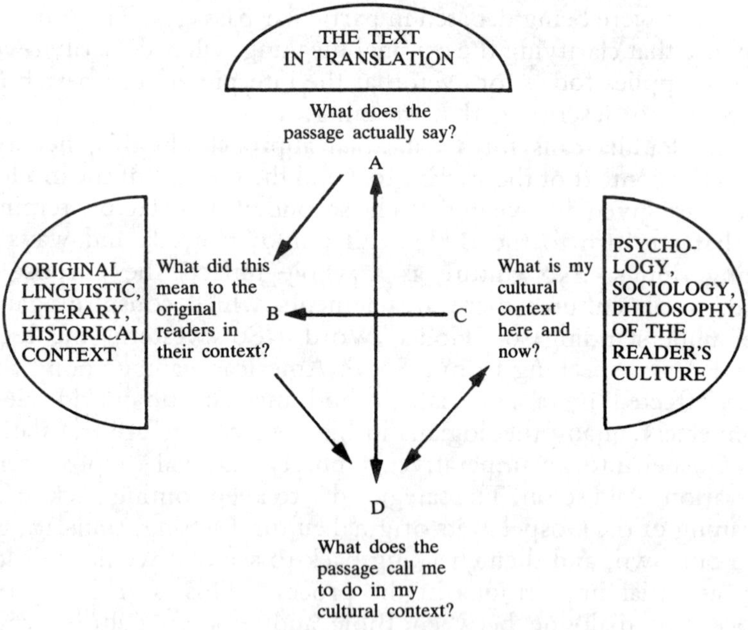

awareness of the two contexts — original (B) and contemporary (C) — which modify the applicability of literal word to contemporary life (D). What Padilla calls the scientific approach tends to take (B) into account but to underestimate the relevance of (C).

The other point the diagram strives to bring out is that the proper outcome of Bible study is action, not just reflection or devotion. What does the passage call me to *do* in my cultural context (D)? There are, for example, some brilliant expositors of the Trinity who won't let a black person into their churches. We must be prepared to respond to the Word with obedience.

Biblical Heritage and Contemporary Experience

We are not yet done with the question of what interplay there should be between biblical content and contemporary experience. The question is usefully discussed by Roger Shinn in *The Educational Mission of Our Church.*[18] Shinn notes that too exclusive a concentration on 'instruction in Scripture, perhaps including Christian doctrine and rules of conduct' can result in learning that keeps 'the power of the Bible at a safe distance from the realities of life'. Conversely, approaches which focus on 'what I am experiencing in my life today', with occasional cross-reference to biblical slogans often lifted out of context, can easily founder in subjectivity.

The answer to this problem must begin not with the issue of content but with the specification of learning objectives, as discussed in the previous chapter. The reader will recall that our general aim is to *draw* persons to God, that they may *grow* in him, maturing in *community* with other believers, issuing in *service* to all persons. It is impossible to interpret these four hallmarks Christianly without turning to the Scriptures at each point for guidance. Nor is it possible to see them being honoured by a curriculum which concentrates entirely on intellectual instruction as the learning environment: relational learning and active witness must be interwoven with it.

It is possible to bring the Bible into a learning experience at any one of three levels. We may simply use a text or passage as lending sanction to a learning activity concerned with some aspect of contemporary service; or we may use it as the source and focus of our learning; or we may draw on the Bible as resource in solving questions of faith and conduct.

Various examples can be given of the use of the Bible to lend *sanction* to an activity. Some preachers merely use a text of Scripture in a literalistic manner as a point of departure, proceeding thereafter to develop favourite thoughts which may bear little or no relation to the real meaning of the text that launched them. There is nothing to commend in this practice. On the other hand, a passage may be quoted (though not expounded) to set the stage, as it were, for a learning session concerned with relationships, or a missionary testimony, or a social action project, or a committee meeting, or some other activity. This is in order, provided that the passage speaks for itself and its relevance to the activity is readily apparent. But the practice will only be valid in a group which at other times has studied to achieve a rounded perspective of biblical revelation. People reared on the use of the Bible for slogans and proof-texts alone are likely to have a magical and unintegrated view of its contents.

The second case is where the Bible is the focus or *source* of the learning activity. The learning objective in this case is to encounter revelation as openly as possible, exposing oneself to the actual meaning of the passage studied and to whatever consequences for thought or conduct flow from it. At a second remove, we may study systematic theology or church history as examples of how other Christians have at various times conceptualised its teaching and attempted to develop a life-style consistent with it. But it is simply not true, as some have attempted to say, that our interpretation of the Bible is inevitably refracted through the current state of theology or churchmanship. These variables do affect us, often more than we realize, and that is why such studies can be valuable in removing obstacles to our understanding of the Bible. Nevertheless, from the scholars of early Antioch to the evangelical scholars of today, there has been a continuous affirmation that the Scriptures in their plain sense communicate a trans-cultural message of reconciliation to the one true God. There is therefore no substitute for direct Bible study, passage by passage and sometimes by theme and over-view, at the heart of a church's teaching programme.

At the same time, it is important to ensure that the authority of Scripture does not get displaced onto the teacher. Bible-centred preachers frequently lack the humility of disciples, offering dogmatic finality as a substitute for an invitation to search the Scriptures for oneself. It is possible for people with a good head-knowledge of the Bible but strong sub-conscious cultural conditioning to tune out unpalatable messages. (One is tempted to quote, say, the racism of the Afrikaans church or the average American Christian's uncritical acceptance of competitive free enterprise as God's own economic theory, were it not for the possibility of a plank in one's own eye!) In biblical interpretation, group discovery is usually more reliable than solo performance since we were meant to mature within the matrix of a fellowship committed to participant learning and the sharing of gifts.

The third way in which the Bible may be put to use is as our main *resource* in solving questions of faith and conduct. Learning activities of this kind begin with a problem and move back into the Scriptures to see what light they shed on the problem. Such problems might relate to anxiety about choosing a career; or discomfort with the views of personality encountered in some kinds of psychology; or the need for a theology of child evangelism, or of general education, or of counselling the dying. Wherever they come from (and the ideal is to find them in the life situations of the particular group of believers), such issues require us to grasp a whole-Bible perspective or set of guiding principles, and then to come forward again and apply the truths discovered to the problem we began with.

In this way we give contemporary experience its appropriate place in our learning. But it was not excluded from the earlier study approach either. Direct Bible-study is meant to produce deeper commitment and a life-style which has become more consistently Christ-like. The problem-centred activity is meant to place the problem under the searchlight of Scripture, again leading to reformation of life. It also needs to be said that issues which arise from focusing on life-problems are often harder to present because a certain minimum level of spiritual (and chronological) maturity is needed if learners are going to know how and where to consult the Scriptures for relevant resources. Problem-centred discussion is not an easy alternative to direct Bible-study, as its apparently more immediate relevance to the learner's present life might suggest. Even with younger children it is desirable to establish in their minds, as an early teaching priority, the general character and drift of the great salvation story.

Biblical Truth and Contemporary Application

Yet one more comment is called for concerning the way we *apply* the Bible to life. Another book would be needed to explore adequately the implications of the complementary processes of interpretation and application, but in the present context I have a duty to suggest some teaching principles that will help learners to become participants in Bible study and not just listeners to other persons' findings.

Clearly the Bible does not speak literally and directly to every situation we are likely to encounter. Its universal message hits home at different levels of generality, depending on how closely the issue in question comes to the personal core of our existence. At the centre, we find basic questions about existence: of a God of purpose, and of human responsibility, redemption and destiny. At this level the Bible is unmistakably direct and explicit. The salvation story transcends its Jewish locality and speaks to all persons of the need and the way of personal restoration.

Moving outwards in concentric circles as it were from this central core (see diagram 7.3),[19] we encounter teachings relating to personal morality and our relationships with others. Much of this material consists of examples in the lives of biblical characters, parables and stories illustrating moral precepts, specific injunctions such as the Ten Commandments, many of Paul's exhortations, and so on. But because the gospel emphasises Christian liberty in the way in which we work out our salvation, there remains great scope for personal judgment after weighing up the facts in the case. Also, we do not live as tribal pastoralists but as industrialised citizens of the technological society, so that the

Diagram 7.3: BIBLICAL TRUTH AND CONTEMPORARY APPLICATION

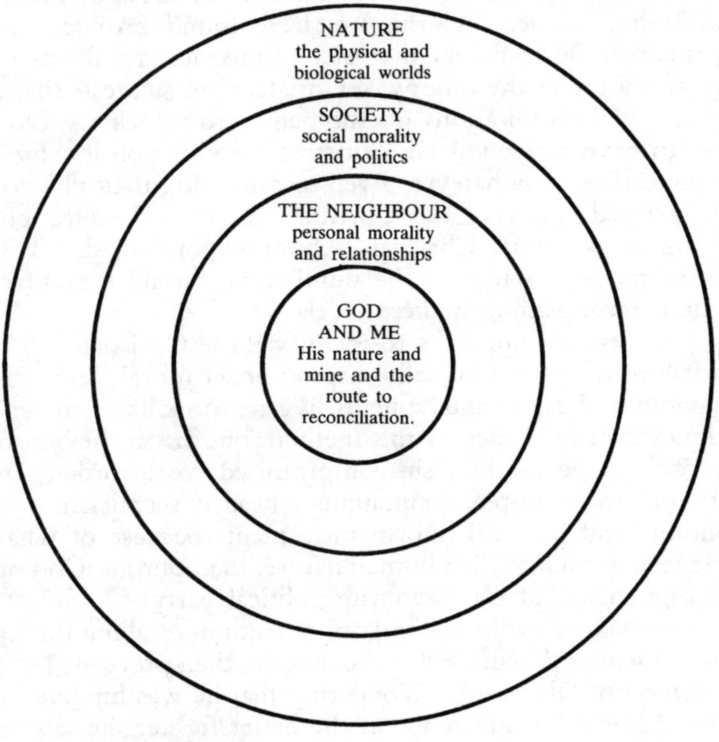

universal principles of morality supplied by the Scriptures need to be interpreted and applied in the light of prevailing cultural patterns. This is the beginning of that applicative skill which John Stott has described as 'cultural transposition'.

The number and complexity of cultural variables increases greatly as one seeks to apply Scripture at the third and fourth levels, namely, to society and the natural world. General biblical principles have to be translated and worked out in social and scientific theories which are bound to look very different from age to age. The wonder — and it is marvellous indeed — is that the Bible, originally written in the language and thought-forms of eastern nomads and farmers, has continued in every era to provide ideas and presuppositions which thinkers in fields as diverse as philosophy, science and the arts have found provocative and informative. But the very diversity of theories and forms which have arisen under the canopy of Christendom suggests that there will always be limitations on the degree to which we can ever claim to have arrived at *the* Christian view of politics, biology, art, education, or whatever. Even to claim dogmatically that we have arrived at, say, *the* Christian theory of education for our time, as some Christian school exponents do, will be presumptuous in view of the number of variables involved in cultural transposition at these levels.

The best we can do is to identify those Christian principles and values which individually inspire, or set moral limits to, our behaviour in these various spheres. We are more likely to generate critiques than syntheses by this method, but that is the best result one could hope for in a sin-compromised world order. One is better off, for example, maintaining a healthy scepticism towards economic and political reform movements because of what the Bible tells us about fallen human nature, than putting God on the campaign ticket of our favourite political party!

John Magee evokes an important truth in recalling the legend that St. George, having killed the dragon, then proceeded to fight the demon of falsehood.[20] Wondering that he was hindered from pressing home his advantage as the better fighter, he saw to his astonishment that Christ himself was protecting the demon. The meaning of this strange thing was that evil cannot be totally destroyed until all the truth which it conceals has been totally revealed. No theological position is totally correct or entirely bankrupt, and those who would mature in their capacity to discern good from evil and truth from error must always keep alert to the possibility that error lurks even in *their* way of stating the truth.

This does not disqualify us from proclaiming some things with joyous certainty, on the authority of Scripture, particularly if they relate to truths at the central core. But it should increase our propensity as teachers to lead learners to the Scriptures, to examine for themselves if what we have said is true,[21] rather than to insist on the rightness of our interpretation. Nor will the most highly trained theologian ever pass the point, in this life, where he or she has no more to learn from simple believers reflecting on life in the light of what they know of Scripture. Maturity is a fruit of body-life.

Footnotes

1. Such as H. Loukes, *Teenage Religion* (London: SCM, 1961); R. Goldman, *Religious Thinking from Childhood to Adolescence* (London: Routledge and Kegan Paul, 1964) and K.E. Hyde, *Religious Learning in Adolescence* (Edinburgh: Oliver and Boyd, 1965).
2. (London: Routledge and Kegan Paul, 1965).
3. *Ibid.*, 70 and 72.
4. H.F. Mathews, *Revolution in Religious Education* (Oxford: Religious Education, 1966) chap. 1.
5. B.V. Hill, ed., *A Charge to Keep* (Sydney: Aldersgate Fellowship, 1971) 28. This and the following two paragraphs largely reproduce what I said there.
6. An international history of this movement is J.C. Pollock, *The Good Seed* (London: Hodder and Stoughton, 1959). The Australasian scene is chronicled in J.R. Prince *Tuned in to Change* (Sydney: ANZEA, 1981).
7. G.R. Rossiter, *Religious Education in Australian Schools* (Canberra: Curriculum Development Centre, 1982) chap. 7.
8. Reported in Hill, *Charge*, 34–42.
9. The latter in the sense that heavy emphasis was placed at all ages on verse-by-verse progress through set passages with little student participation or activity.
10. E. Schaeffer, *L'Abri* (London: Norfolk, 1969) 227.
11. The archives of Bible Societies abound with attested cases. See also D. Winter, *For All the People* (London: Hodder and Stoughton, 1967) and J.B. Phillips, *Ring of Truth* (London: Hodder and Stoughton, 1967).
12. As C.S. Lewis points out in his devastating professional criticism of the approaches of people like Tillich, Vidler and Bultmann, in 'Modern Theology and Biblical Criticism', in his *Christian Reflections* (London: Geoffrey Bles, 1967) 152–66.
13. This position is lucidly represented in A. Richardson, *The Bible in the Age of Science* (London: SCM, 1961). Compare also what he says about Barth, 89–95.
14. See J.M. Hull, *School Worship: An Obituary* (London: SCM, 1975).
15. R. Padilla, 'The Interpreted Word: Reflections on Contextual Hermeneutics,' *Themelios* 7:1 (Sept, 1981) 18–23.
16. *Ibid.*, 19.
17. The term 'hermeneutical circle' has been used in a variety of ways. Basically it refers to the philosophical, psychological and cultural factors involved in the interaction of text and reader. See A. Thiselton, *The Two Horizons* (Exeter: Paternoster, 1979).

18. (Boston: United Church, 1962) chaps 2 and 3.
19. This diagram and explanation first appeared in my *Faith at the Blackboard* (Grand Rapids: Eerdmans, 1982) introduction.
20. J. Magee, *Reality and Prayer* (London: Hodder and Stoughton, 1958) 82–83.
21. The Bereans were commended for doing this in order to check the validity even of what the great Paul himself was saying. See Acts 17:11.

8

Learning Environments and Resources

The first step in planning our teaching ministries in the church was to remind ourselves of the biblical vision of the whole person maturing in Christ. The second was to assess the needs of our people, discovering the particular sub-sets of needs, consistent with this vision, experienced by various groups in our congregation. We were then ready to draw up, in consultation with the members themselves, learning objectives for a teaching programme. Chapter six worked through these issues.

Now the question arises: which learning environments are most suited to achieving these objectives? This is the point at which, as chapter five reminded us, the standard curriculum theories fail us because they tend to take for granted that we will operate with trained teachers in school classrooms. The argument of chapters two and three, however, was precisely that this kind of learning environment, while useful for some purposes, is quite unsuitable for others. We also noted that biblical writers in both testaments looked to quite different contexts of learning to achieve the object of teaching the law of the Lord.

This is not to say that we should reject out of hand the possibility of using the schooling model for some of our purposes. Radios and films didn't feature in biblical times either, yet we would be foolish to reject their possible uses in Christian nurture and evangelism. The crucial thing is initially to keep an open mind on the question of what learning environments are most likely to lead to the fulfilment of our objectives.

What options are available to us? Provisionally, let us identify them as homes, churches, schools, entertainment and mass media venues, and outdoor settings. Each of these categories is capable of sub-division, depending on a variety of factors such as the status of those who perform teaching roles in each of these settings, and the style of instruction it is thought proper for them to adopt. Let us take each in turn.

The Home

We have seen how firmly and unambiguously the Bible makes parents responsible to immerse their children in a knowledge and understanding of God's word. Nor is there any room to subject this principle to cultural transposition or to delegate the responsibility to the church or the school. The Bible entertains no prospect of primary family relationships giving way to other forms of human association. If they do not survive then society as such will collapse. There is mounting sociological evidence to substantiate this conviction.

It seems then that parents, for good or ill, are teachers. What parts of our objectives for children and youth are capable of being fulfilled through home influence? Psychological studies are confirming that many basic responses are laid down in the early years of life, even before the child is old enough for kindergarten or pre-school. If we take the seven areas mentioned earlier in diagram 6.1 as representing the *scope* of our objective statements, it can be seen that the home has an impact on every one.

For example, first, the *cognitive* capacities of human beings require an adequate foundation of stimulating and varied experiences in early childhood, coupled with rich language development. Children who are shut away for long hours in bedrooms with a dull or static decor to suit the parent's convenience become cognitively undernourished. If, in addition, their parents rarely address them, or do so impatiently or with inattentive baby-talk, they will be slow to develop a vocabulary to think and speak with.

Secondly, *affective* capacities need similar opportunities for exercise and extension. Feelings colour the world for us and sharpen our perceptions. The basic pleasure/pain feelings exhibited at birth rapidly become differentiated by experience into positive and negative ranges of feelings, likes and dislikes, interests and aversions. An important area of feeling is empathy, the capacity to 'feel with', to enter imaginatively into the personality and experiences of other persons. Children starved of personal contact and play with others, or forced by some trauma into shutting off their capacity to empathise, become secretive and introverted. In pathological cases they become criminals who show no remorse or capacity to identify with the hopes and hurts of others. Such can be the damage done in a child's life before it reaches school age.

In the third place, *dispositions* are obviously likely to be affected by patterns laid down in early life. And to the extent that they incline the individual towards certain habitual forms of behaviour, they are hard to alter once they are implanted. Homes characterised by mutual criticism and whining, for example, produce adults who complain and criticise less from intention than from habit.

Fourthly, *self-esteem* has deep roots in home life. No other environment (with the possible exception of the second home one sets up as a parent) is so important for enabling the individual to believe that he or she has worth as a person, irrespective of the level of achievement in the world outside. Frowned on by a teacher for obtaining a low mark in some school subject, the discomfited child comes home, hopefully, to the place where it is loved and recognised for its own sake, irrespective of its achievements. Tragically, there are parents who either neglect or ignore their children in the pursuit of adult pleasures, or transfer their own unachieved goals and competitive spirit onto the shoulders of their children, commending them only when they win glory for the family.[1]

Fifthly, the home either increases or inhibits the child's capacity to enter into caring *relationships* with other persons, and to seek the satisfactions of interpersonal experiences. The child bruised by uncaring relationships at home enters the world with a serious handicap, which affects not only its dealings with other persons but its understanding of God. Who, knowing their father only as a selfish domineering bully, will adequately grasp the notion of God as our heavenly father? Many youth workers find themselves engaged in difficult remedial work with young people warped by their home experiences.

Sixth and seventh in our list are the home's provision of a most appropriate context for *gift-development* and the assumption of *responsibility* for various tasks in the family environment. Unfortunately, many parents are too lazy and too dependent on labour-saving devices to expect contributions from their children to the good order and entertainment of the family group. The consumer society, and the isolating habit of constant TV viewing, have turned many homes into boarding houses where each member fulfils private plans without taking others into consideration. The father having abdicated his role of team leadership, it falls often on the mother to be the only one who sets aside her personal objectives to perform the duties that minimally 'keep the home going'.

The biblical home, by contrast, is a small community which cherishes interaction, frequently worships together 'the Father from whom all fatherhood in heaven and earth derives its name' (Eph 3:15)[2] and discusses his law. All members experience loving discipline and mutual service, rejoice in each other's achievements and share each other's burdens. The Christian home is a prototype of the body of Christ, though not completely so, since it is unlikely to exhibit a sufficient range of the diverse gifts of the Spirit promised to congregations, especially if it is restricted to nuclear family size.

Does this mean that parents should train as teachers? Yes and no. Since many of the learning objectives we cherish for children are most effectively met in good home environments, and since the task of coping with the pressures of modern society is complex, we do need to take steps to help our believing parents to understand their roles Christianly. Parenting courses should be given high priority in the learning church.

At the same time it would be a mistake to try to professionalise the parent role and bring into the home the structures of formal teaching. Some parents invest considerable time in tutoring their children systematically in various skills thought to be important in an achievement-oriented society. Women's magazines often present instructions for 'raising your child's I.Q.' or 'making your child a fast reader' which ambitious mothers eagerly follow. There are parents who push their children remorselessly to 'do their homework (or music practice)' to the point where they impair the friendship that is possible between parent and child.

It is rather sad that in a compendium of essays on 'Evangelical Christian Education', only the last of thirty-two chapters is conceded to the topic 'The Home as an Educational Agency',[3] but the chapter itself, by Morris Inch, is insightful. Inch captures the spiritual perspective of human family in the remark:

> In a deeper sense than we know, parents are God's representatives and representations to children. They appear godlike, and God seems to the child parentlike. Early childhood knows little of right or wrong, but much of what parents like or dislike. Eventually the child comes to realise that even these godlike parents fail and fall short. On these occasions the parent must be repentant and ask forgiveness. Thus the child "may learn that God is someone much better and more wonderful even than the parents. Secondly, he may learn that, when he has done wrong, he too must ask forgiveness of God, and of other people if he has done them wrong". The parent is the child's first step toward God, but the decisive step is one of personal faith in Christ as Saviour.[4]

Parenting courses, home study groups, and leaflets for children to take home to their parents are some of the strategies that can help to restore the proper participation of parents in the teaching ministry of the church. But parents are to be approached as equals, not pupils. One writer has noted that research shows that few parents open and use the parenting material sent home for them.[5] The probability is that much of this material has the look of schooling upon it, and that immediately raises the defences of many adults. The same writer notes, however, that the minority of parents who do actually use such materials are people who have responded to study opportunities and parenting courses in their churches.

Perhaps we can make up ground by dissociating parenting from the formalised teaching role which the schooling model has fixed in their minds. As Emil Brunner has remarked:

> The Church is not an educational institution, but it is the community of the redeemed. . . Even the father who prays with his children and reads the Bible with them acts not as an educator but as a 'priest', not in the 'world' but in the 'church'.[6]

Teaching in the home is best characterised by spontaneity and example. Events in family life provide opportunities for the glancing remark that exemplifies faith. Discussing news of the day, problems and discoveries, opens the way to praise or prayer. For example, it is good that the family Bible reading at meal-time should be frequent, but not to the point of being invariant at all costs so that duty replaces delight.

Again, Reuel Howe describes with great sensitivity how an eight-year-old girl, cross with her mother, cuts up with scissors a party dress her mother is making to wear that night. The mother discovers it, and crumples weeping on the bed. The daughter enters and sees what she has done. 'Mummy?' she whispers, but gets no reply. 'Mummy please?' she begs. Her mother replies ungraciously 'Please what?' 'Please take me back,' is the plea. The mother reaches out for her, unconsciously typifying God's atoning action, and forgives, even whilst admitting that she had perhaps failed to spend enough attention on her daughter. She too needs forgiveness. Thus, says Howe, 'the daughter's experience now has a meaning that will help prepare her for participation in God's atonement'.[7]

The special challenge of the home as a learning environment is to pace the development of the child from dependency to autonomy. The home is not an entirely voluntary context of learning, since parents have duties of upkeep and control to which children must submit. Yet part of nurture must involve encouraging independence and the acceptance of responsibility. These objectives don't suddenly come into focus at the onset of adolescence. They should be in our minds from the earliest, so that little by little the child learns self-determination. Small tasks well performed lead on to bigger responsibilities. The parent welcomes the signs of independent self-hood which, while reducing the parent's ease of mastery, increase the possibilities of easy friendship with one's own children.[8]

The home is the cradle of the church's teaching ministry, and the church must keep coming back to it. It must, for example, relish the opportunities for teaching inherent in the NT emphasis on Christian hospitality. I remember the gratitude of an older church member invited to an evening to farewell another family leaving the district. This active church member had never been inside another member's home! By contrast, the NT is a continuous chronicle of what happened in home meetings, ranging from study groups to casual encounters.

One pattern which has proved helpful is that of encouraging groups of three to four families with children to meet as extended families in each other's homes every two or three weeks for *family worship*, with the host family providing the informal teaching segment after a meal together, and leading the time of conversational prayer amongst those present. The pattern has had unexpected spin-offs, with older couples and single adults being drawn in to fill out the pattern of an intergenerational extended family. It has been found that members tend to keep in touch during the week because they have begun to care more deeply about what happens to the others.[9]

The Church: Its Forms of Life

The second primary context for Christian teaching ministries is the church. But a great deal depends on the meaning we attach to the term 'church'. Interpretations range from those which emphasise visible denominations with hierarchical structures dispensing the mystical rituals of their tradition, to those which declare the church convened whenever two or three are met together informally. Biblically the truth lies between these views. The Scriptures use the Greek word *ekklēsia*, usually translated 'church', in two contexts. One refers to the total assembly of believers in all ages, whose membership is known only to God, and there is no hint that any one visible structure on earth would have a membership approximating to church in this sense.[10] The other is a far more common biblical usage, and identifies particular local assemblies or congregations of Christians. Fraternity between congregations, not union of them, is all that can be inferred from the biblical documents.

Another term occasionally used for the body of believers is 'household' (Gk: *oikos*),[11] of which Christ alone is the head. The connotations of this word are warmly familial and, perhaps, warrant the description of a healthy congregation as *an extended family of extended families*. It is the image we need in order to understand the kinds of learning environment we should be striving to create in the church: not the formal, schooled arrangements of parallel pews in front of a preacher, reminiscent of the traditional classroom or lecture hall, but the informal, lived-in atmosphere of a family living room where it is easy to contribute to the common activity.

How the believers of the NT congregated together seems fairly clear, although centuries of ecclesiasticism and church architecture have tended to cloud our vision. The emphasis was on community, the sharing of a common life-style, derived from the apostles' teaching (Acts 2:42, cf. vv.6–14). The first church, in Jerusalem, alternated large gatherings for worship and teaching, initially in the temple of Herod, with small-group fellowship and sharing in each other's homes (Acts 2:46). The original apostles taught in both settings. 'Day after day in the temple courts and from house to house, they never stopped teaching and proclaiming the good news that Jesus is the Christ' (Acts 5:42). There was, as Snyder puts it, 'a winsome freedom from dependence on buildings'.[12] When the temple ceased to be a safe venue for Christians, and the faith spread to other cities, the larger gatherings were held in large homes, hired halls or the open-air as circumstances dictated.

Some Christians today, fleeing from clericalism and denominational bureaucracy, have pinned their hopes entirely on small groups. But the NT shows us a pattern in which small and large groups were necessary and complementary.

The *large group* has its uses. But how large? The thousands meeting together in the first flush of the church's emergence seem in later biblical documents to have dispersed and multiplied in smaller congregations dotted all over the Mediterranean world. There are still congregations in many parts of the world, such as South Korea and South America, which number many thousands of members, but it is probable that there is a point beyond which healthy congregations must sub-divide to save their members from becoming passive fellow-travellers lost in the mass.

The lower limit is determined by how many people it takes to generate a diverse and balanced expression of the spiritual gifts described in such passages as Romans 12, 1 Corinthians 12 and Ephesians 4. The large group is able to bring to focus gifts of organisational leadership in such areas as teaching, evangelism, training, specialist counselling and social service. These are exercised with a view to helping every congregational member to discover and develop his or her special gifts, exercising them in 'works of service'. Snyder, writing in a country which worships bigness, makes the surprisingly modest estimate that a congregation of 'a few hundreds' is probably sufficient for these things.[13] After that, it is time to sub-divide and establish a new residential focus for a second congregation.

This rough estimate has some plausibility in the Australian context. There are examples of congregations of this size which have proved able to support agencies to help the sick and the needy, social action groups, and several missionaries in other places, almost at the level of a small denomination.

The large group is able, then, to use to the maximum the leadership the Spirit of God gives to some members. It can also provide a setting for skilled biblical teaching and high moments of corporate worship. Small groups can be very vulnerable to eccentric individual emphases, and need the corrective of large-group oversight.

The *small group* provides for the more intimate, extended-family caring and gift-sharing that I mentioned earlier.[14] At various points in church history this configuration has restored vision to the church, providing a crucible for problem-solving prayer and Christian growth, and inspiring various forms of mission to society. Typically, in the NT such groups were intergenerational, and some of the excitement in current experiments with congregational forms comes from rediscovering the familial warmth of intergenerational fellowship. The basis of some people's criticisms of conventional Sunday school approaches is their strict segregation of the age groups. I will indicate in a moment why I do not regard this criticism as entirely valid, but there is no doubt that the tendency towards generation gaps in our culture has not been resisted strongly enough by the churches.

NT patterns were intergenerational because people tended to use their homes as their work bases, the family responded to social demands and changes as a unit under the authority of its male head, and 'teenagers' hadn't been invented. The child became an apprentice-adult as soon as it was able to help mother, father or craftsman on the job. And adulthood was marked off by recognition of discussion rights amongst the elders. For the Jew this came at the age of thirty.

Have things changed so much in the present era that these biblical precedents need radical cultural transposition? I suggest that the large group and heterogeneous small group structures have a transcultural validity because they reflect unchanging principles in the biblical revelation. The large group, big enough to co-ordinate the spiritual gifts, small and local enough to remain an organic community of believers; the heterogeneous small group, big enough to benefit from extended family diversity, but small enough to care and share intimately: these seem necessary minima for any group claiming to be a church in the biblical sense, and they remain viable even in our technological mass society.

It is possible, however, that more disposable kinds of association may be needed in addition to these basic forms, to help Christian people to cope with particular features of contemporary life. One is the increasing diversity of roles each individual is called on to play in any one week. We customarily eat and sleep in one place, work in another, study somewhere else, fraternise with a different group for our physical recreation or hobby, and worship with yet another. We meet different people in each place and are, in some respects, different people ourselves. The pressing need is to remain committed Christians in each context.

Nor can the age differential be ignored. The nature of the industrial economy separates the child from the adult and creates an intermediate sub-group called adolescents: neither children, because they are physically mature and capable of abstract thought, nor adult, because the workforce can not yet absorb them. Added to this are the forms of age segregation practised by schools, based mainly on chronological year of birth. Moreover the commercial media are labouring indefatigably to beam the market appeal of their goods to these different age groups, fostering the myth of a teenage sub-culture to sell their wares. It is possible that their efforts may eventually turn the myth into reality because after much repetition we are beginning to believe what we are told.

The upshot of such developments is that the individual Christian encounters problems and challenges in relation to the separate roles which he or she is required to take on during the week. This generates a demand for small homogeneous or *common interest groups* of two kinds. One is the study-action cell geared to the problems of different age-groups (such as primary school children, lower secondary school children, upper secondary youth, working youth, etc.). The other is occupationally related (such as nurses' Christian fellowships, campus fellowships and industrial fellowships).

Our century has seen a mushrooming of such groups; some within local church or denominational structures, others alongside these structures, and for that reason often called *para-church* organisations. It is not uncommon to find church pastors and denominational leaders referring rather disparagingly to the latter, as though they were competitors for the loyalties of Christian people. This is ironic when one considers that these same leaders constantly urge their people to go out and be witnesses to their faith during the week. It would betoken a healthier pastoral concern if they were to invite their members to report back to their churches on their involvements in witness and para-church fellowship during the week, in order to recruit each other's prayers.[15]

Each of the three types of group I have so far mentioned tend, to varying degrees, to have a continued existence. The most durable is the large group or congregation as such. The next most durable are the smaller heterogeneous groups, though internally they may experience significant changes in atmosphere as individual members or families move on, and others join in. The third type, small homogeneous or common interest groups, tend to change composition fairly frequently because members are moving up the age range, switching from study to work, or changing jobs. But the structures survive the turnover of their parts because, and only so long as, they meet a need.

The fourth type of group is the ad hoc *task-force*, formed for a specific and usually short-term purpose. It is not to be regretted that everyone in the same church is not fired up by a particular community action project such as involvement in local schools, care for the elderly, opposition to a local council policy, home visitation, or operation of an evangelistic communications unit. Depending on gifts, God calls different people to different works of service. The duty of the rest of the congregation is to know of the involvement of their members in such projects, and to support them in prayer.

It should be noted that none of the groups I have described was convened specifically for educational purposes. Teaching and training ministries of some kind are inherent in all of them, but the teaching is imbedded in praxis. It is now time to look more closely at the types of specific teaching activity most suitable in each configuration.

The Church: Appropriate Learning Environments

Preaching

The vast majority of Christians rely mainly upon the input of a preacher at weekly mass worship for their understanding of the faith. Earlier, I defined 'preaching' as teaching for commitment. It involves the clear presentation of the basic rationale of faith, the central salvation story, with a strong invitation to respond to God in the ways implied by that story. Understood thus, preaching is not an activity confined to the pulpit during weekly mass worship. But that is the context with which most people associate it.

This is unfortunate, since the average pulpit — 'six feet above criticism', as someone has put it — owes more to the class distinctions of medieval society than to the spontaneous proclamations of itinerant apostles in the NT. The formality of the occasion also inhibits asking questions for clarification, or discussing the accuracy and validity of the preacher's interpretation. We now live in an age where many preachers, influenced by critical fashions in theology or their cultural conditioning, need to be called to account for the truths they proclaim. It is also an era in which the education of many congregational members will at least equal that of the ministers, justifying a greater employment of dialogue rather than declamation, and a greater use of the gifts of lay preachers.

A further problem presented by the mass preaching situation is the difficulty of catering for the diverse needs and interest levels of a heterogeneous congregation. Various improvements on conventional practice may be suggested.

(a) The preacher may assist hearers to grasp the content of the preaching by issuing a summary of points for them to follow, or by displaying them on an overhead projector.

(b) The congregation may be encouraged to follow references to and exposition of Scripture in their own Bibles or, alternatively, in an agreed upon new translation as readily available to them as hymn books now are.

(c) The preacher's message may be followed within the mass worship time or in a subsequent study time by opportunities for questions and comments, and perhaps small discussion group follow-up.

In one sense, such suggestions are tinkering with the problem, given the limitations inherent in the attempt to teach many people simultaneously. Admittedly, the very gifted preacher can often surmount these limitations to a surprising degree. But it may be questioned whether we should require anyone to do so, especially since such people are comparatively rare, and the sound teaching gifts of others are discouraged by reliance on the solo performer. More radical modifications are possible.

(d) One or two other congregational members gifted in teaching ability may be invited to respond to the preacher's presentation. This structures the response a little more, and may be improved by the preacher giving the respondents some prior notice of his theme and outline. The intention is not to call for criticism of the preacher but wider sharing of insights relating to the topic. In fellowship, no one need feel defensive or pretend infallibility.

(e) The main teaching segment may be transferred to an age- and interest-grouped study programme *before* the mass worship time, leaving the latter to focus more devotionally on all-age praise and celebration (I will say more on this pattern in a moment).

The two main obstacles to the introduction of such modifications to traditional patterns are congregational and clerical resistance. Regarding the first, many people draw comfort and courage from traditional practices, even when they may be defective and sub-scriptural. It is insensitive to try to force changes on people without adequate explanation and persuasion. The wise innovator will preface attempts to alter things by discussing the issues in sermons and committees before changes are made. The body must decide, not single members (not even the clergyman).

Secondly, some clergy become defensive at such suggestions because they have been conditioned by their training to see their role in medievalised autocratic terms. Yet, as chapter nine will point out, their particular range of gifts, training and full-time availability make them the ideal people to (i) monitor the teaching heart of congregational life, and (ii) draw out and train the lay preaching gifts present in their congregation. There need be no fears that clergy will lose role-definition in a learning church.

Beyond the Sunday School

The second area of reappraisal must be what in many churches is called the Christian Education Programme, based mainly on the conventional Sunday school model. It will be recalled that chapter three expressed reservations about the schooled mentality which can so easily creep into teaching ministries in this area, and chapter five detected shortcomings in the traditional model of curriculum development associated with schools. To these criticisms must be added the observation that adults are inclined in many churches to dissociate themselves from group study opportunities because they assume that just as school is for children, so is Sunday school. Ought we then to dispense with Sunday schools?

Let us not be too hasty. What have been the merits of the Sunday school idea? First, in the past it has provided a more systematic teaching coverage of the salvation story than most other church activities. Secondly, it has responded to developmental considerations by adapting the presentation to the understanding and experiences of different age-groups. We noted earlier in the chapter that the complexities of modern society require opportunities for nurture in more homogeneous groups. Thirdly, it has capitalised on the teaching advantages of small groups using a variety of learning resources. Fourthly, it has often had an evangelistic opportunity with regard to children from homes where the parents, though not themselves committed to Christ, are anxious to expose their children to Christian values. Perhaps the wisest way forward is to modify rather than to discard.

How can we become more Judaeo-Christian in our Sunday school practice? The first essential is to confirm the primary responsibility of the home by building our staffing around *parental involvement*, as well as using other congregational members with teaching gifts. There is almost a case for saying: don't let professional teachers take over. The trained teacher has a place in the church's teaching programme, just as the theologically trained clergyman has. But it is less one of doing the teaching than of training the lay members to use their general ability to help learners.

The second essential is to modify our approach to curriculum along the lines suggested in chapter five. Thus we will seek to involve the learners in identifying their own needs and participating in the formulation of objectives. We will also encourage *participant learning*, where each teaches the other rather than one authority teaches the class. We will also encourage joint evaluation of the programmes, and the disposition to respond to what has been learnt with deeper commitment and social action.

The last point leads on to an emphasis, thirdly, on *response and responsibility*. We will discourage the idea of learning for its own sake, and will try to link the study programme in with the worship and witness of the members of the body.

In this respect it is not inappropriate to contrast the Sunday school idea with another great nineteenth century approach to Christian nurture, through the Christian Endeavour Movement. As conceived by Rev. Francis Clark in Portland, Maine a century ago, its principles included stressing commitment through the taking of a pledge and the monthly consecration meeting and making every member responsible for some particular task through a committee system and various forms of community outreach and service. Teaching came to be guided through age-graded, biblically balanced topic books, which helped to train young members to share the task of presenting the studies. The participant learning climate of a C.E. meeting was a distinctively different experience from being in a Sunday school class.[16]

Finally, we need to emphasise that all believers are learners, and have something to gain from *group study at all age-levels*. This has been the thrust of that particular modification of old patterns labelled the 'All Age Sunday School'. For reasons given earlier, I regard the name as unfortunate. Some other churches have achieved a better image with 'Lay Training Institutes', 'Christian Study Programmes' and other such titles.

It may be useful to describe one pattern which attempts to bring together points made in this and the previous section. Church X has a Christian Study Programme on Sunday mornings for all ages. Each level is staffed with two co-ordinators and a roster of adult helpers, mostly parents, who serve for roughly a third of the year in the younger levels, spending the rest of their time as participants in the adult study programme. Within each level, the children span about three school years, and are divided into three or four mixed groups. Each group is associated with a couple of adult helpers, and together they prepare one main teaching segment for presentation about once a month. A typical session will include 10–15 minutes in small groups with general conversation about the past week and some preparation for a future main teaching segment; then the main segment for the day, presented by one group to the whole level; then back into groups to do follow-up activities or prepare a future segment.

The youth and adult levels of the Christian Study Programme roster members to lead whole group or small group studies as the occasion warrants. A *training schedule* for developing different skills and ministries operates through the year, serving the needs of this and other church programmes.

Following the C.S.P. and a brief break is the Family Service, focusing on all-age celebration and intercession. The teaching segment in this service picks up the common theme running through the sessions of the C.S.P. for that day and builds a worship experience around it. There is considerable involvement of families and lay talents in this reverent but informal gathering of the body.

At other times in the week, church X has a number of *common-interest* groups, including social and outreach elements in the youth programme, and a *task-force* operating a centre for activities for the elderly. It also has a pattern of all-age groups convening in each other's homes for *family worship* as described earlier in the chapter. From the point of view of the church's teaching ministry, each of these activities contributes to a balanced curriculum and cannot be thought of in isolation from the other facilities the body provides for its members.

Catering for Youth

A special comment is needed regarding the provision we make for youth. Some churches tend to mimic broader social patterns by segregating youth in a self-contained programme, and then blaming them for poor patronage of the conventional service of worship on Sunday. Ignoring the teaching value of being given progressively wider responsibilities, they also deny them effective access to the church's decision-making bodies.

A healthy church's contact with youth will be at many levels, corresponding to their own levels of awareness of God and his people. Homogeneous groups of various kinds will be needed, offering such activities as (i) social interest evenings; (ii) study-coaching services (for those taking examinations); (iii) community service task-forces to utilise the skills of the unemployed; (iv) training programmes of various kinds; and (v) prayer-study-action cells or 'disciple groups'. Indeed, given the amount of (often enforced) free time that young people have, many churches are seeing the priority they need to give to maintaining an around-the-week facility for youth, in which organised activities such as the above grow out of developing informal contacts. Such ministries cannot be sustained without the involvement of a sizeable group of committed youth and adults undergoing regular training.

At the same time, the healthy church will constantly work at drawing youth into the more family-oriented parts of its programme. Not only do they not see the church if they stay exclusively within a youth programme, but they miss out on the adult models essential to development in this transition period of life. Staid congregations locked into conventional older styles of worship must be less unyielding to the expectations of those who will lead tomorrow's church. Family worship groups must take extra pains to draw into their circles those youth — an increasing number — who are effectively parentless and suspicious of adults in general.

Furthermore, the presentation of the faith to youth, while it should include emphasis on the achievement of self-identity, should do so not in a context of mere entertainment or instruction, but through sharing in Christian body life and the call to witness and service. Many young people are *in* the church but not *of* the church because we have not drawn out their gifts or given them genuine responsibility in the body as a whole.

The Mass Media and Entertainment Venues

The third possible range of learning environments listed at the beginning of the chapter was the mass media and entertainment venues. It is a fact of modern life that much education, for good or ill, occurs through entertainment as mediated by commercial interests. Amongst voluntary youth organisations there is growing concern about the number of unattached youth who prefer the freedom conferred upon them by affluence and private transport to commitment to a group. They are the target of skilled entrepreneurs who will advertise any preposterous stunt or perversion thought likely to attract a voyeurist youth audience. The result is mounting immoralism in the community.

What will the Christian faith-community do about this? It is clearly hopeless to try to compete directly by attempting to produce an equal amount of professional counter-entertainment. Some individual Christians will be called to conquer the world of entertainment, and may thereby have the opportunity to register a public vote for the Christian option. If there are such in your congregation, they will need continual careful support (as opposed to disapproving frowns). At less professional levels, gifts in drama, music, dance, painting and other arts deserve encouragement and a place in the church's worship and teaching experiences.

It is part of our teaching ministry, however, to help our people, young and old, to get their values straightened out, and to develop a critical awareness of what the media are trying to do to us. Three responses will be inadequate. The first is to ignore the problem and hope church activities will crowd out the alternatives. This ostrich reaction will simply make the church appear irrelevant. The second is to condemn the media and preach abstinence. This ignores the fact that much valuable learning as well as innocent pleasure can be gained from them, provided we are aware as well of the hazards. Similarly, the opposite reaction of totally accepting their contribution to our cultural life without grappling with the challenges they present to a Christian life-style is lazy and dangerous.

We must help our members to maintain a continuous Christian critique of the values and life-styles encountered in the mass media and entertainment venues. As always, this must begin in the home. Parents need to foster in their children a disposition to discuss the things they see and learn in other places, so that spiritual discrimination will develop. The writer to the Hebrews identifies the disposition that is wanted: 'solid food is for the mature, who by constant use have trained themselves to distinguish good from evil' (Heb 5:14).

This may happen when the family watches a television programme together. Someone asks as the set is switched off: 'Well, what did you think of that?' Or, rather than condemn some notorious and widely acclaimed show, parents accompany their older children to it and, again, discuss it afterwards.

Similar things can happen at church level. Preachers may from time to time give or invite Christian critiques of acclaimed films, books, and shows. Youth groups may attend entertainment venues and afterwards be led through a discussion of the life-values they saw represented there. The church must come to terms with the fact that the cinema, the television set, and, most potently, the transistor radio, have achieved a dominance over people's discretionary time that has never been known before. We must foster critical awareness from a Christian perspective.

It may reasonably be asked whether there should be a heavier investment by the churches in religious advertisements and broadcast programmes? One may well become sceptical in cost-benefit terms about the huge outlay required for mass media access, and feel that we will have to await the advent of closed-circuit television to obtain opportunities tailored to our budgets. Better returns may be possible from generating articulate consumer awareness in our churches and protesting steadily at the media use of extremists or ecclesiastical dignitaries to represent the religious views of the Christian community.

The cost-benefit problem does not seem to arise in relation to what some writers are calling the 'electronic church'. Opinions on the merits and likely impact of this growing phenomenon (already remarkably powerful in the USA) are divided.[17] Televised studio church services can generate their own income. It is another question whether they generate Christian conscience and community. To people wooed by the spectator consumer mentality in so many other areas of life, these programmes are likely to have similar appeal. It is important that our aim of fostering critical awareness with respect to the media extend to these programmes too. Churches could profitably arrange to view various religious programmes and then have study-discussions on their merits with members of all ages.

Outdoor Settings

It is a mark of urban civilisation that we manage rather effectively to insulate ourselves from the powers and wonders of nature, thereby depriving ourselves of a witness to the living God (Rom 1:20). Sometimes they enter our living room through some of the well-documented nature films which appear on television, but this is still a literally denatured experience compared with the smelly, tactile, three-dimensional reality. There are possibilities in natural settings for learning-experiences of awe, meditation, and a sense of finitude and eternity which lead spontaneously into reflections on fundamental questions. Christ and the prophets were adept at seeing 'sermons in stones' and 'heaven in a wild flower'.[18]

Family picnics and church outings, hikes and river treks, orienteering, nature rambles (to observe flora and fauna systematically) and camps are some of the many possibilities. What kinds of learning do such settings foster? A glance back to diagram 6.1 shows that such activities can cover the whole range in a whole-person way.

In particular, group activities in informal natural settings give youngsters an opportunity to see adult leaders in more informal, life-related behaviour. It is a misuse of the opportunity if a highly structured, formal programme is superimposed on the time available. Friendship, reflection and deep sharing take time to develop. It is also wise to enter into a pact at the outset that the distractions of a noisy technological culture — radios and television in particular — will be left behind.

Camps which run for several days are more effective than rushed weekends in building relationships and relaxing taut personalities. They can often, however, pose greater problems of discipline, especially with youth from unsatisfactory home environments. It is part of a Christian witness to maintain a just society in camp, so misbehaviour cannot be condoned. But the aim of developing voluntary relationships obliges us to tread carefully in maintaining control and in requiring participation in religious exercises.

For example, Christian camps usually seek to set the tone of a Christian life-style by having daily studies which explore the salvation story at a level of awareness appropriate to the participants. In cases where that awareness is rudimentary, the use of small group Bible study and discussion may be felt to be threatening and oppressive. It might be better to depend on direct talks or visual aids which may reasonably be included in the obligatory timetable, while offering voluntary opportunities for group or individual discussion.

The greater scope in such settings for consecutive teaching, group leadership and personal counselling will be wasted or abused if our teaching ministries do not include specific training for such roles. *Many churches assume that just by throwing people together in informal settings, people will relax, see what has to be done, and do it effectively. That is a naive assumption*, and causes many an activity to fall short of achieving its objectives — if, indeed, any objectives were actually spelled out when initial planning began!

Learning Resources

In an earlier day the learning resources of the church were basically the Bible in vernacular translation, the question-and-answer approach to Christian knowledge enshrined in the catechism, the symbolism, art and drama incorporated in church architecture (as much determined by cultural as biblical values) and the liturgy and rituals of the particular denomination. This is no mean list!

In the present day, educational technology presents us with an astonishing range of materials for all ages and most interests. The problem is to be sure that the glamour of some book, learning package or curriculum kit does not disguise a poverty of theological depth and biblical perspective. As we said in chapter five, it is unwise to start examining such resources until we have first determined our learning objectives, appropriate content (in general terms) and preferred learning environment. It is useful to set up in a congregation a *curriculum review committee* which utilises the available expertise of clergy and trained teachers to monitor the quality of the resources it is proposed to use in the church's various groups. A check-list of evaluative criteria is proposed in diagram 8.1.

A question not raised in this check-list is whether the teaching aids called for in the materials under review require technology you do not possess. There are many technical aids that now tend to be taken for granted. A minimal range of equipment likely to be needed in a good modern teaching programme is listed in diagram 8.2. The list is far from exhaustive. It does not, for example, include super 8 and 16 mm movie projectors, which are pleasant to have but not essential to most curriculum kits and in any case less flexible in use than slides and film clips or strips. Television gear is not mentioned, though now widely available. Much occasional equipment can be developed using imagination and local materials, and a good curriculum pack will make many useful suggestions along these lines, not all favouring the child inclined to a literary-academic kind of response (see check-question 12 in diagram 8.1).

Furniture: The Hidden Agenda

A final word on learning environments and resources concerns architecture and furniture, the hidden curriculum in many churches. Most church buildings themselves owe so much to medieval antecedents that they are hard to use for purposes other

Diagram 8.1 *CHECK-LIST FOR EVALUATING CURRICULUM RESOURCES*

PERSONAL OBJECTIVES (See chapter 6)

Do these materials satisfy needs:

1. Identified in our chosen learning objectives?
2. In ways that encourage learners to set and achieve their own objectives?

BIBLICAL BASIS (chapter 7)

Do these materials approach the Bible:

3. As central source or peripheral resource?
4. Magically, analytically or in a sceptical spirit?
5. In ways that foster the users' desire and ability to study the Bible for themselves?
6. In ways that reveal appropriate applications to contemporary faith and life?

CULTURAL RELEVANCE (chapters 4 and 6)

Do these materials communicate:

7. Meaningfully to our church members in this culture?
8. Relevantly to their life in this society?

TEACHING METHODS

Do these materials use teaching methods which:

9. Address our prospective learners at the right intellectual and developmental levels?
10. Arouse and maintain interest?
11. Encourage self-teaching and gift development?
12. Utilise several forms of response, e.g. listening, viewing, discussing, expressive art forms, worshipping, serving others?
13. Invite curriculum evaluation?

TECHNICAL PRESENTATION

Are these materials:

14. Rigidly prescribed or able to be used flexibly for our purposes?
15. Accurately and attractively printed?
16. Complicated or easy to follow?
17. Durable, at least for the length of the programme?
18. Reasonably priced and within our budget?

Diagram 8.2 A MINIMAL EQUIPMENT LIST

* Chalk and chalk boards.

  and/or
* Overhead projectors plus transparency rolls and overhead pens.
* Cassette tape recorders.
* Film-strip (or clip) and/or slide projectors, 35 mm.
* Piano or other musical instrument to accompany singing and movement.
* A photocopying facility able to reproduce printed sheets, overhead transparencies and duplicator stencils.
* A duplicator — ink or spirit — plus stencils and paper.
* Butcher's paper rolls and masking tape.

than clergy-centred liturgy or lecturing. Many of the cultural-ecclesiastical values of former times are incorporated in the vestments worn, the areas it is traditional for lay people not to enter — at least during services — the communion rail holding the laity back from direct access to the table, the submissive formality of parallel pews, the vested authority of raised pulpit, even the seclusion from the world outside achieved by high, tinted windows. All these things convey messages about the Christian faith and its relation to the world and to authority. This hidden curriculum may be working against our very attempts to be biblical in our teaching ministries.

At least, if rules and sentiments limit our ability to modify the lay-out of the main venue for large-group worship, we may exercise some initiative in arranging and equipping other areas for teaching and meeting. But one piece of advice will perhaps prove difficult: let us try to avoid giving our premises the appearance of school classrooms or characterless boxes with merely chairs in them. See what can be done with open spaces, cushions, couches, bean bags, sturdy armchairs, and pot plants to simulate the family atmosphere of the living room at home.

Group the seating in configurations which serve the particular purpose, avoiding straight rows at right angles where possible. Seats in circles, curves and clumps will break the tendency to formality which inhibits spontaneous contributions. Even in a large auditorium, seating rows which tend to a semicircle are to be preferred to straight series.

Such comments may seem trivial in a study more concerned with re-conceptualising the field of teaching in the church, but they are meant to illustrate the subtlety with which older ecclesiastical and current pedagogical attitudes can be represented in our programme. Even the arrangement of furniture can work for or against us.[19]

The most heretical suggestion I could make, in the eyes of some Christians, but one consistent with the NT is, of course, that instead of trying to simulate family-style learning environments in churches, we should use the real thing and meet in homes. At least for small group activities, such learning environments cannot be bettered.

Footnotes

1. See also F.F. Wise on 'The Family' in *Exploring Christian Education* (ed. A. Elwood Sanner and A.F. Harper; Grand Rapids: Baker, 1978) 148–51.
2. Variant reading (NIV).
3. By M. Inch, in *An Introduction to Evangelical Christian Education* (ed. J.E. Hakes, Chicago: Moody, 1964) 404–18.
4. *Ibid.*, 405. The quotation within this quotation is from L. and W. Brown, *The Christian Family* (New York: Association, 1959) 37.
5. J.C. Wynn, 'The Home and Christian Education', in *An Introduction to Christian Education* (ed. Marvin J. Taylor; Nashville: Abingdon, 1966) 299.
6. Quoted in J.M. Swomley, Jr, *Religion, The State and The Schools* (New York: Pegasus, 1968) 66.
7. R. Howe, *Man's Need and God's Action* (New York: Seabury, 1953) 132–37.
8. See B.V. Hill, *A Teenager is Many People* (Sydney: ANZEA, 1970) chap. 2.
9. Useful resources include D. Purnell, *Working with Families* (1980) and K. Pearson and I. Allsop, eds, *Family Activities: A Collection of Resources for Intergenerational Groups* (1977) both published by the Joint Board of Christian Education of Australia and New Zealand; and the discussion booklet *The Christian Home*, by R. Heynen (Grand Rapids: Baker, 1975). See also B. Narramore, *Help! I'm a Parent* (Grand Rapids: Zondervan, 1972) [plus his *Guide to Child Rearing*].
10. Such is probably the sense of Matt 16:18; Eph 1:22; 5:22.

11. As in Gal 6:10, Eph 2:19, 1 Pet 2:5. For an insightful discussion of the biblical basis to this model, see R. Banks, *Paul's Idea of Community* (Sydney: Lancer, 1980).
12. Snyder, *Community*, 147.
13. *Ibid.*, 123.
14. There is a rich quarry of theory and suggestions for small group operation in the series produced by J. Mallison as *The Small Group Book Series* (Sydney: Renewal, 1976).
15. There is a deeper irony in such criticisms from denominational authorities, because our survey of biblical usage indicates that, strictly speaking, denominational structures themselves are para-church, and by that definition usable or disposable according to cultural need.
16. The C.E. Movement is still strong, though tending to hang on to nineteenth century *procedures*, mistaking them for the sound biblical *principles* they then enshrined. Here too, in the author's view, the way ahead is to modify rather than to discard.
17. See the useful range of views in *On Being* 8:2 (March 1981).
18. William Shakespeare, *As You Like It* (Act 2, Scene 1) and William Blake, 'Auguries of Innocence'.
19. Malcolm Knowles, an adult educator, doesn't think it unimportant and makes a number of useful comments in Knowles, *Adult*, 133–56 and 174–77.

9

Guiding the Church's Teaching Programmes

At the beginning of chapter six I raised the question whether a general model of Christian personhood could be found in Scripture from which specific learning objectives could be derived for the church's teaching ministries. We studied one of the many possible passages available, and obtained a commission to *draw* persons to God, that they might *grow* in him, maturing in *community* with other believers, and issuing in *service* to all persons.

This indicates that a great deal depends on the effectiveness of the faith-community as a nurturing agency. A church which relies upon well-bred formality once a week as its primary style of fellowship is likely to produce staid, sallow Christians. A church which depends on the teaching output of one overtaxed member, even if he be a highly trained and talented clergyman, will produce spiritual starvelings who fall away when their patriarch goes to another charge. Is there a Scriptural model of fellowship that can guide our approach to teaching structures?

The reader will undoubtedly be ahead of me, if only because such a model has been frequently touched on in previous chapters. Again, the NT provides us with an embarrassment of riches. John Stott reminds us that most of the images used have OT antecedents. The church is the bride of Christ, the vineyard tended by the divine gardener, the flock led by the great shepherd. Four other principal metaphors bring out more strongly aspects of human responsibility: the Kingdom of God, the family of believers, the building under construction and the body of Christ.[1]

The last of these — the body of Christ — has the greatest yield for pedagogic purposes, because it puts the various members of the body at each other's service as they 'teach and counsel one another with all wisdom' (Col 3:16). Significantly, as Stott points out, this is the only image with no direct OT equivalent. The priesthood stood in the way of such an image of the people of God in the OT, but in the NT, Christ is the head of the body and we are all members. With unusual sharpness Stott remarks:

> It is only against the background of the equality and unity of the people of God that the real scandal of clericalism may be seen. What clericalism always does, by concentrating power and privilege in the hands of the clergy, is at least to obscure and at worst to annul the essential oneness of the people of God. Extreme forms of clericalism dare to re-introduce the notion of privilege into the only human community in which it has been abolished.[2]

We saw in chapter three that to this offence, historically, has been added a secularised version of the same thing — professionalism. Shaw anticipated the kind of soul-searching that people such as Ivan Illich have provoked in the present day when he made a character in *The Doctor's Dilemma* say: 'All professions are conspiracies against the laity'.[3] Special skill in performing a *function* tends to be given special *status*, leading to a consequent reluctance to allow others any longer to perform that function without professional licence. Thus are the gifts of people smothered by jealousies. A great non-Christian, A.N. Whitehead, was aware of this situation in human affairs generally when he remarked: 'Very few people are adequately drawn out. . . the waste of undeveloped faculties must be tremendous'.[4]

One Body, Many Gifts

If it is sad that such a state of affairs exists in a fallen world, it is scandalous when a church reflects the same situation. The metaphor of the body and its members implies the utilisation of gifts, by all, for the good of all. In saying this, I do not want to be interpreted as denying the value of professional training or advocating the abolition of the clergy. The body of Christ has much to gain from both, but there is need for Christians in both categories to leave behind worldly ideas of status and power and to reconceptualise their proper service to the body.

Again it is useful to look at the passage in Ephesians chapter four on which we drew earlier for our model of Christian personhood.

> There is one body and one Spirit . . . But to each one of us grace has been given as Christ apportioned it. This is why it says: 'When he ascended on high, he led captives in his train and gave gifts to men' . . . It was he who gave some to be apostles, some to be prophets, some to be evangelists, and some to be pastors and teachers, to prepare God's people for works of service.

We are here reminded that there is one body, many gifts; one Spirit, many ministries.

Snyder suggests that 'for generations the subject of spiritual gifts was largely misunderstood or ignored by much of the Christian church'.[5] Latterly there has been an upsurge of charismatic spirituality which has brought back to the consciousness of many Christians the weight attached in the NT to the exercise of spiritual gifts in the body of Christ, but sometimes at the expense of, in Snyder's words, 'elevating one or two gifts to the level of spiritual ID cards.'[6] There is a suggestion in the passage under study of two categories of gifts. Snyder speaks of 'a functional distinction between the basic leadership or enabling gifts and the great variety of other, more specific gifts which the Spirit gives'.[7] But this should not be pressed too far. Other biblical passages offer variant lists, though some enabling roles reappear consistently, as may be seen from diagram 9.1.

The main lesson to draw from comparisons of these gifts[8] mentioned in these various passages is the fluidity of the concepts. One can loosely distinguish three levels of ministry. These were, first, people with enabling gifts who ministered in the one congregation. Variously called teachers, elders, overseers, pastors,

Diagram 9.1 THE GIFTS OF THE SPIRIT

Rom 12	*1 Cor 12*	*Eph 4*	*1 Pet 4, 5*	*1, 2 Timothy and Titus*
	apostles[a]	apostles		
prophecy	prophets	prophets		
		evangelists		
		pastors, shepherds		overseers (*episkopoi*)
teaching	teachers	teachers	elders (*presbu-teros*)	elders
taking the lead	administrators			administrative helpers (*diakonos*)
serving (*diakonia*)		(to prepare God's people for works of service)	serving, ministry	
encouraging, exhorting			speaking for God	
giving to those in need				
showing mercy				
	able to help others			
	healing			
	tongues — speaking			
	interpreting			
	speaking with wisdom[b]			
	special faith			
	miracle-power[c]			
			hospitality	

a. Occurring 81 times in the NT, Snyder shows its usage was not confined to the original 11 apostles, *ibid.*, 86–89.

b. W. Barclay distinguishes the word of wisdom (*logos sophias*) as knowledge of God through thought and communion, from the word of knowledge (*logos gnōseōs*) as practical application to life in *The Letters to the Corinthians* (Edinburgh: St. Andrew's University, 1956) 127.

c. Supposed by many to be the exorcism of evil spirits.

administrators or helpers, they obviously constituted a team of people leading their church together. By the time of the writing of the Pastoral Epistles, some of these functional descriptions appeared to be settling down into descriptive titles of a broad kind, though still more suggestive of function than hierarchical position. And leadership was still exercised through a group rather than a monarchical individual.

A second group of people with enabling gifts was itinerant, moving between churches and exercising no over-arching function of control, except that the original apostles of Christ were unique monitors of the church's teaching. Both enabling groups existed to draw out the ministries of all believers, amongst which the same gifts could appear in more specific ways. Thus, for example, prophecy, evangelism, teaching and serving each appear sometimes as enabling ministries, while being mentioned at other points amongst the general ministries of Christians.

As regards specific gifts, the descriptions become so varied and fluid that there seems to be no good reason to assume either that the list is complete or that those mentioned will necessarily occur in every age and congregation. Also, the gift of 'serving' or 'ministering' is open to a wide range of applications, and justifies our extending the list of possibilities for today in the directions sampled by the questionnaire in chapter six.[9]

Clearly, it is unlikely that any one person will turn out to be gifted in all these ways. Hence churches dependent on solo-performers, clerical or lay, are out of step with Scripture and almost certainly defective in worship and witness. Secondly, every member has some spiritual gift to contribute to the health of the whole body. We cannot afford to dismiss anyone as inessential or unremarkable. As a young teacher with rather intellectualist pretensions in a country appointment, I learnt this lesson from the retired farmer's wife who regularly offered me Sunday hospitality. She would have laughed to hear herself described as gifted, but in spiritual terms she undoubtedly was. And so are we all if we respond to the Spirit.

This gift-sharing applies even to preaching and pastoring, now often regarded as the distinctive prerogatives of ordained clergy. *Applying biblical truth* to modern living needs the perspectives of both the clergy with their ability enhanced by training to expound what the Bible says, and the lay people striving to live biblically in secular employments. *Pastoring* people in our complex, stressful society calls for many kinds of gifts, to deal with death, depression, unemployment, domestic boredom, work pressures and a host of other differentiated pastoral needs. In both areas, highly educated and skilled lay people are multiplying in number, and can ease the unnecessary loneliness and overwork in which many clergy have let themselves become trapped.

Enabling Ministries

It becomes apparent that the enabling ministries of the church to its members are intended to make them in turn *mature ministers*. Peter did not assure the believers that they had become a chosen people *with* or *under* a royal priesthood; he said: 'You *are* a chosen people, a royal priesthood, a holy nation, a people belonging to God, that you may declare the praises of him who called you . . .' (1 Pet 2:9). Each clause is an alternative way of describing the whole body of believers. Each person is chosen to be a priest mediating the good news to the world.

Hence the line becomes blurred between *teaching* and *training*. We are never teaching people merely in order to assist their own spiritual development. We are simultaneously equipping them for service to others. We have not discharged our teaching function if we have merely imparted doctrine and exhortation. We are responsible to indicate areas of application and to link them with witness-training. The further implication is that those who manifestly have the talent to lead, teach and pastor large groups of people will also be drawing out other potential enablers.

This is where a functional kind of hierarchy should develop in a church, provided members retain their humility and willingness to interchange functions. For example, where the congregation has called someone with formal theological training to serve their faith-community full-time, they should have the expectation that that person will both *teach* systematically the revealed word of God, and *train* others to do the same. Hence lay preachers ought not to be viewed as emergency stop-gaps for the minister's crowded preaching schedule, but as necessary gift-sharers in the life of the congregation.

The preacher who is unwilling to draw out people with gifts similar to his own and to share with them the benefits of his own training, as is the case with many clergy, is in the wrong faith-community. 'I believe I have been called to preach', said one clergyman to the author, thus seeking to excuse his refusal (or inability?) to train others for that ministry. He seemed to be unaware how unscriptural his attitude was. He could not see that rather than being threatened by a potential loss of function and status, he was being invited to give the faith-community a more bracing kind of leadership, partaking less of the image of the mystically set-apart executive director, than that of the playing coach.

Clerical appointees are also usually expected to perform a substantial pastoral function, though training in Australian theological halls tends to skimp on the kinds of study most needed for this kind of ministry. Still largely in fealty to the literary-academic mode of learning, colleges are prone to neglect or to assign low status (for assessment purposes) to the therapeutic disciplines and to clinical experiences under supervision. Many congregations contain trained counsellors and social workers who could transfer their skills to spiritual pastoring very readily, and train others to do the same. The mature clergyman will welcome their presence in the team, both in helping him to pastor and in drawing out the potentials of others in the congregation with similar gifts.

This suggestion leads on to another point which has also been touched on in earlier chapters. It is not only clergy who suffer from a sub-scriptural view of their role in the faith-community. It is also professional teachers. And in both cases the confusion is aided and abetted by the average congregation, conditioned to see itself as a flock of amateurs led by trained professionals. One is very likely to find trained teachers in churches assigned to teach small classes of children, when by rights they should be training others to use the basic teaching skills the situation calls for. We have already noted that the ideal teachers in the church family are parents rather than professionals. It is also not unusual to find such people, given a little expert help, doing the task with measurably greater enthusiasm than those who have been teaching professionally all week.

As for other trained professionals, such as the psychologists and social workers already mentioned — plus youth workers, health professionals, managers and accountants — churches rarely see how they too could be passing on relevant and valuable skills to fellow-members whom the Spirit has touched with gifts of pastoral and administrative service. Forsaking the elitism of the Greek model of professionalism, those who are professionally engaged in secular life should serve their home congregation by training others in the same skills for the upbuilding and expanding of the whole body.

It must also be admitted that a third class of believer is likely to have a sub-scriptural view of its role in the faith-community. The average congregational member, when approached, tends to be reluctant to take on responsibility or undergo training. Sometimes the pace of modern life or the temptation in the consumer society to use one's leisure selfishly prompts the individual to plead that he is too busy. Alternatively, the combined effect of experiences of failure in academic subjects at school and years of passive pew-sitting in church produces a sense of personal inferiority which results in people seeing the invitation to exercise their gifts as threatening rather than liberating. Rome wasn't built in a day; nor are effective patterns of body-life in the church achieved overnight. The attempt must be made, however, for the sake of both the church and the world.

Administrative Structures

All this talk about drawing out people's gifts and calling on suitable persons in the congregation to exercise enabling ministries implies that in any congregation which has grown beyond the size of a small group there will be a need for administrative structures. So let's get down to practicalities.

Some Christian people shudder at the mention of the word 'administration'. It conjures up in their minds images of dull committees and authoritarian adults. Often, young people in particular feel that spontaneity is the key and committees a thing to be avoided. Such attitudes confuse liberty with laxity. Administration is, after all, one of the gifts of the Spirit (1 Cor 12:28)[10]. The important thing is to make the structures serve the goals and not let them become sacred in their own right.

Who, then, will carry out the administration? Our discussion of spiritual gifts made it clear that the healthy church will not be limited to the gifts of one person. Unfortunately, for reasons given previously, the assumption is too often made that the clergyman is the logical person to be the chief administrator. Many churches lay such heavy burdens of administration on the clergyman that his time for study and preparation is squeezed out and his teaching becomes superficial and unreflective.

The Star Turn

Let us imagine pastor X coming to a new appointment. The congregation is small and accustomed to letting the minister do everything. Isn't that what they pay him for? The two Sunday services are completely in his hands. He is expected to keep the membership list up-to-date and visit each family at reasonable intervals. Church business meetings are chaired by him, and other programmes expect him to look in from time to time and, perhaps, take devotions. There is a women's group which, though it does not expect him to be its leader, presumes he will have married a suitable candidate! There is also a Sunday school which he will have to superintend because the local Christian school teacher has just been transferred. The position in which pastor X finds himself is very like diagram 9.2.

One can catch glimpses in this pattern of NT features: but *only* glimpses. There are, for example, Christians meeting together in large group format for teaching and worship. The nurture of the young is getting some attention, and a scattering of elders periodically discusses policy. Essentially, however, it is a clerical-star system. Everything revolves around the clergyman. His days are filled with administration, visitation and exhortation, possibly in that order of priority.

Diagram 9.2 A CLERICAL-STAR SYSTEM

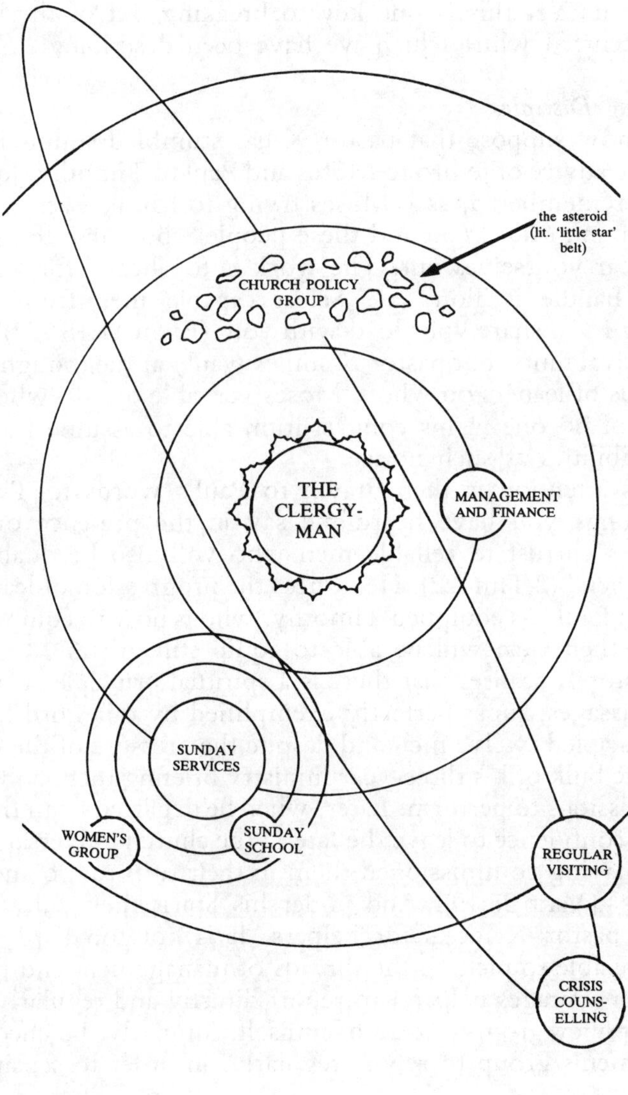

If one were to suggest that pastor X add to his roles that of *trainer*, the very thought would be burdensome, and even threatening, given that his theological training did little to prepare him for it. Yet this is one key to breaking out of the kind of clergy-centred whirl which we have been describing.

Recruiting Disciples

Let us now suppose that pastor X has stumbled simultaneously upon the advice of Jethro to Moses and Paul to Timothy. Jethro, it will be remembered, saw Moses trying to handle everything on his own and said: 'You and these people who come to you will only wear yourselves out. The work is too heavy for you; you cannot handle it alone . . . Select capable men from all the people . . . to share your load with you' (Exod 11:18–22). These are survival hints, but pastor X smiles wanly at the thought of the hundreds of leaders on whom Moses was able to call, whereas he knows of no one in his congregation able to assume leadership responsibilities at such notice.

His attention is then drawn to Paul's words to Timothy: 'The things you have heard me say in the presence of many witnesses entrust to reliable men who will also be qualified to teach others' (2 Tim 2:2). He notices the progression of leadership training: Paul has equipped Timothy, who is now to equip others, who in their turn will be able to equip still others.

Pastor X realises that there is a spiritual principle at work in these passages, most perfectly exemplified by our Lord himself. Jesus discipled twelve men and despite the pressure of the crowds spent the bulk of his three-year ministry briefing them and giving them missions to perform. Later, when he departed from them, he had the confidence to leave the fate of the church universal in their hands, having commissioned them in their turn to 'go and make disciples' (Matt 28:19). And under his Spirit they did.

So pastor X looks for helpers. It is not too hard to find someone able to pick up the threads of management and finance, and he encourages helper 1 to report directly and regularly to the church policy group instead of himself. Similarly, he encourages the women's group to report regularly, in order to sensitise the policy group itself (called by different names in different denominations) to the duty of spiritual oversight which they had previously left with the pastor.

Next, pastor X finds someone willing to help in arranging the weekly worship service with him. Part of his regular preparation now involves meeting with helper 2 (sometimes by phone) to indicate his Bible readings, general theme and possibly a preferred song, from which helper 2 develops a worship sequence and leads the service. Pastor X cherishes helper 2's willingness to be a sounding board and invites criticism of his messages. In return, he works for the time when helper 2 will be sufficiently equipped to preach the Word and train others for similar roles in large-group worship activities.

Meanwhile helper 3 has consented to co-ordinate the Sunday school under pastor X's guidance, freeing him of direct administrative load though he is still involved to some extent in teaching. Both of them work to identify other adults who can help, using team teaching rather than one adult per class to help people gain confidence and learn on the job.

Another helper has agreed to assist the pastor in commencing a weekly evening for youth. Again, it is needful for them to meet fairly regularly together to discuss opportunities and problems. Helper 4 is also seeking to draw in other adults who can relate to young people. They recognise that with many young people in the district alienated from their homes, the church policy group needs to work quickly towards the appointment of a youth worker who will be able to maintain a centre for contact open for most nights of the week, through which opportunities for counselling and small group teaching can be developed. But a clergy-centred congregation can't quite envisage that sort of arrangement yet.

Indeed the congregation doesn't at first notice anything particularly different in the church's life. Administratively, the basis has changed from a clerical-star system to a clerical-support system, but it still revolves around the clergyman. He is still constantly 'up-front', and were he to leave or fall sick, the activities of the church would falter very promptly.

But like yeast in the loaf, significant changes are on the way. The pastor is gaining strength from his helpers and is spending much time with them. They are disciples, with whom he seeks to share his skills. And they become friends whose concern for him pastors the pastor. He seeks identification with them, not a distancing from them, and this requires self-exposure on the model of the apostle Paul who told the Thessalonians: 'We loved you so much that we were delighted to share with you not only the gospel of God but our lives as well' (1 Thess 2:8). He meets with this whole group every so often, often with spouses included, to share his ideas and plans for building up a more effective form of gift-sharing body-life. He has ceased to think of it as 'my church' and speaks constantly of 'our people'.

Pastor X's load has not been lightened, but the priorities have shifted. Others bear it with him, and the nurture and equipping of other 'enablers' has assumed central importance. Compare diagrams 9.2 and 9.3 to see the distance we have come.

Developing Ministries

While all this is going on, pastor X becomes conscious of a change in his helpers. When he first drew them together, they were all fairly typical 'simple believers' following his lead. But he now begins to discover in them robust spiritual resources of which even they had not been aware. Some disappoint, but in others responsibility and encouragement bring out strength of character and gifts.

Nearly all clergy (and others) find certain aspects of their role hard to perform. People's strengths differ. Pastor X, for example, feels particularly useless and inarticulate when visiting elderly people. At first he feels he must not reveal his sense of inadequacy about this because his people expect him to be perfect. But his support group is more realistic, and he finds himself admitting the problem to them. One immediately volunteers to help. She turns out to be wonderfully suitable to minister to elderly people. Humanly, pastor X feels a twinge of jealousy, until he realises that he is not Christ. The master-disciple model only tells part of the story, for in another sense we, including pastor X, are all disciples

Diagram 9.3: A CLERICAL-SUPPORT SYSTEM

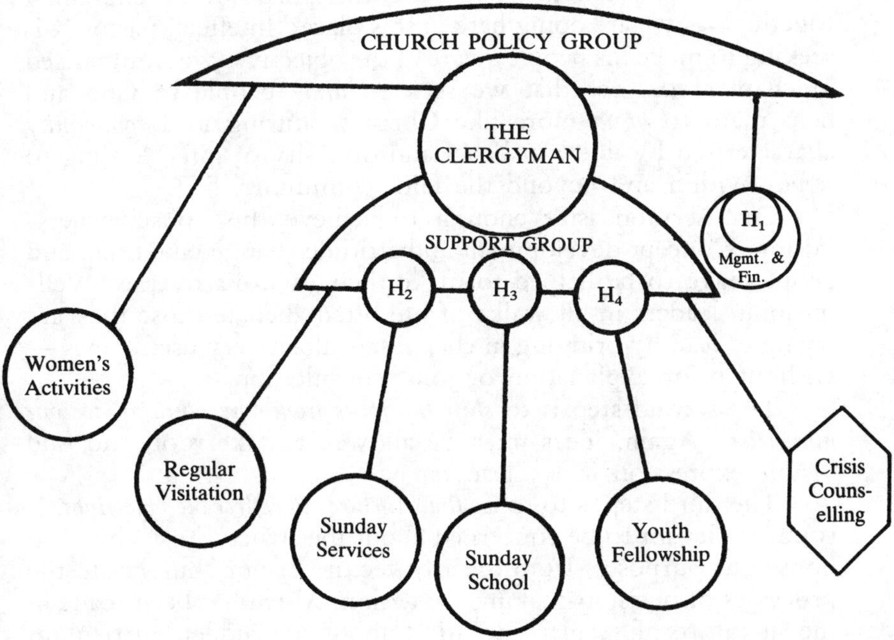

of the one Master. So we need also the more egalitarian model of body-life analysed at the beginning of the present chapter. The pastor is one of a team, and some of the good players are catching up on the coach.

Again comes the twinge of apprehension. But he is beginning to have confidence that this earnest group of co-workers will never think less of him for building others up to their full potential. It is those who aspire to status of the worldly kind, riddled as they are with self-interest and pride, who have reason to fear that others will rejoice at their mistakes. As he prays the matter through, pastor X commits himself to awakening all his people to their potential ministries. But how?

The first step is to *raise the congregation's level of consciousness* by teaching them what the Scriptures reveal about the nature of faith and church life. Against a background of NT perspectives, pastor X raises the question: 'What are the purposes of churching together[11] as we are doing here in this place?' In effect, pastor X is seeking to make his people aware of the objectives we summarised in chapter six, i.e. that we seek to *draw* people to God and help them to *grow* more like Christ; maturing in a *community* characterised by unity in belief and diversity of gifts, leading to *service* within and beyond the faith community.[12]

One sermon isn't enough to achieve this consciousness-raising. Concept development and attitude change take time, and people have to be helped to make their own discoveries. Well-meaning leaders in all walks of life often alienate those they are trying to lead by bringing in changes — albeit very useful ones — without prior explanation or joint consultation.

The second step is to *shift the focus from 'the minister' to 'our ministries.'* Again, ideas must be allowed to take root, and find visible expression in lay leaders.

The third step is to *revise the structures to reflect the objectives*. It is not irrelevant to be concerned about the structures we build to house our purposes, from the architecture of our churches to the processes of decision-making we design. Much has been made in the literature of secular education about the hidden curriculum which lurks in such structures. Messages are conveyed by whether we worship in fixed pews or movable seats, for instance, or by whether there is genuine prayer in our business meetings or just a formal benediction to sign off as it were. Pastor X sets about to replace the 'clerical-support system' of diagram 9.3 that is entrenched in people's minds with the alternative sense of church structures being a 'congregational support system'. This does not call for an immediate drastic re-designing of every group in the church, which would probably be very disruptive and cause anxiety. Pastor X builds on what is already there. Let's follow his reasoning, as depicted in diagram 9.4.

First, pastor X calls on his helpers to come a little 'higher' and work alongside him as co-leaders in a *committee of ministries*. This is a management group, not a legislative body, so it does not have to be large and representatively elected. But it does need to

Diagram 9.4: A CONGREGATIONAL-SUPPORT SYSTEM

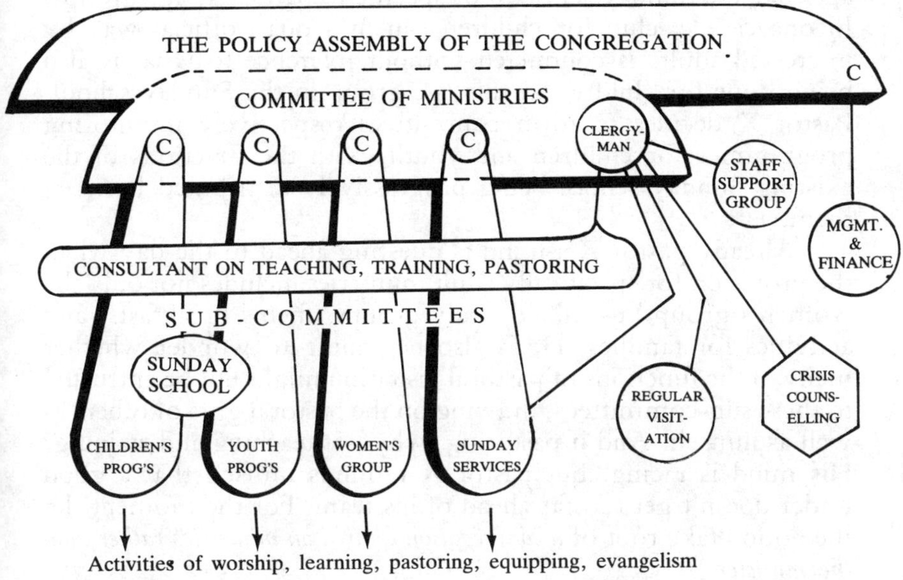

report back to such a group — a policy assembly of the congregation — constituted according to the rules of pastor X's denomination. The unfortunate thing about much church government is that it does not separate policy-making and general oversight (for which a large body of believers *is* appropriate) from detailed planning and co-ordination. The committee of ministries is there to co-ordinate and generate programmes helpful to the body of believers in a variety of ways. The helpers have now become convenors of sub-committees working at the grass roots.

But what sub-committees are needed? Pastor X doesn't want to cause unnecessary upset by changing the names and operations of groups as yet. He strives instead to help people to relate their functions more consciously to the objectives of the fellowship. He had wondered about setting up committees on worship, education and mission, but he is rightly apprehensive that this might separate activities which were meant to go together.[13] He notices, however, that existing activities in his church tend to be either all-age (like the Sunday services) or specific to particular age groups. In one case, a club for children run in a quasi-official way by interested adults is conducted without reference to what is also being done for children in this age group in the Sunday school. Pastor X decides to form committees respectively monitoring programmes for children and youth, with the functions of the existing Sunday school being progressively distributed between them.

Already pastor X's mind is questing ahead to the day when the provision for specifically adult ministries includes not only the women's group but mixed study groups, men's breakfasts, and activities for families. He is also beginning to wonder whether many of the functions of pastoral visitation might not be entrusted to these sub-committees, drawing on the pastoral gifts of others as well as himself. And if pastoring, why not teaching and training? His mind is racing, but pastor X reminds himself that a good leader doesn't get too far ahead of his team. For the moment, let the notion take root of *a congregation centred on ministries rather than the minister.*

Big Can Remain Beautiful

All that has been said so far is applicable to the typical small church. But the number of concerned and equipped people in pastor X's church is growing, and an inevitable consequence is general growth. Pastor X finds his committee of ministries developing functions which reduce its availability to be an intimate support group for him. He therefore draws such a group around him on a more informal basis outside the administrative framework.

Meanwhile, the greater number of people concerned about the needs of youth in the church produces a problem of co-ordination and strategic planning which calls for another full-time worker in the congregation. But can the church cope? One member with a flair for financial management points out that if the fifty wage earners in the congregation set aside a fifth of their weekly tithe for the purpose, the sum produced would be a wage which was the average of all their salaries.[14] There are other factors to consider, of course, but this bit of realism reduces the general sense of paralysis at the sum involved, the church goes to prayer, and they are moved to take the step.

Church growth is more rapid. Pastor X is busier and wonders whether after all small was beautiful. He is also suffering some very human withdrawal symptoms as the youth worker and gifted laity gain increasing visibility at his expense. But he sees that the answer to both feelings is an even firmer commitment to developing the gifts of all. And in doing so he earns not the disdain but the gratitude and respect of those whom he is helping to maturity. They are eager to lighten his load, and in this intention they are aided by a further rationalisation of the administrative structure of their congregation.

An Administrative Lattice

Let us now jump ahead to the point where the congregation has grown to the 'few hundreds' which Snyder considered optimal.[15] There is no one right way to organise a congregation, but one possible structure is shown in diagram 9.5. To the pastor of a small inner-city or rural church it may look unattainably grandiose, but it is entirely compatible with the smaller model shown in diagram 9.4, and provides a possible target to aim for in the long term, whilst still accommodating further growth. It incorporates the following principles.

1. *Committees are programme-oriented rather than function-oriented.* There is a recognition that churches strive to meet needs, and some needs are specific to one's time of life — whether child, youth, or adult. At the same time, the strong familial flavour of NT Christianity prompts us to encourage complementary all-age programmes as well. Within this category, the *all-age worship committee* monitors the regular large-group celebrations of worship and core teaching; the *family networks committee* services a network of small groups each consisting of from four to six families and friends (elderly folk and young singles) doing things together.

Diagram 9.5: A BODY-LIFE SUPPORT SYSTEM

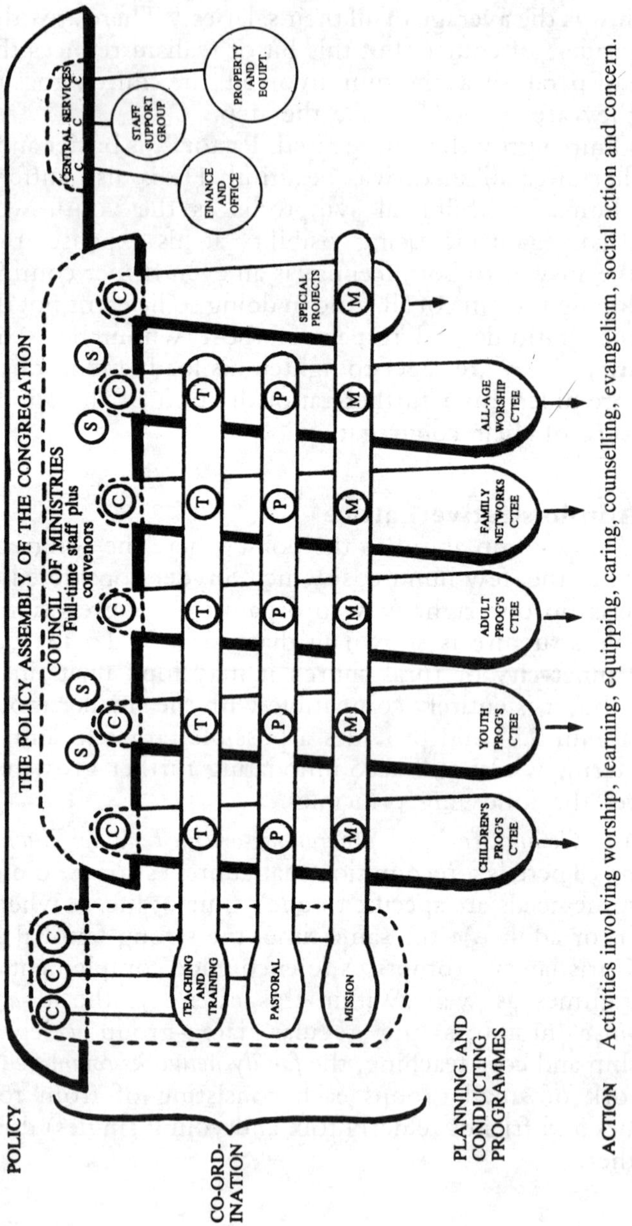

2. *Each programme links learning and doing.* There is no programme committee whose responsibility is confined exclusively to worship, teaching or mission. Even the all-age worship committee strives to encourage worship and teaching which are meaningful at all levels, whilst also featuring the witness and actual work of its members. Prayers of intercession pick up not only the needs of the people but their activities, work-settings and witness in para-church organisations during the week. Also featured are the special projects which the church itself is sponsoring.

The concept of Sunday school has receded, though specific opportunities for age-based group study have never been better. The programmes for children, youth and adults each have a concern for systematic learning, through Sunday classes for some, disciple groups for others, and special courses for others again. Such provisions are seen not as self-contained but as part of a rounded programme for that age-band, and one that is geared to equipping the Christians for ministry, not just spiritual security.

3. *Co-ordination of functions and planning is built into the structure.* This is what creates the lattice effect. Programmes flow downwards; mechanisms of oversight and co-ordination flow across. The council of ministries is itself one of the latter. It keeps itself informed of plans and activities throughout the fellowship, monitoring the whole for duplications and areas of neglect. In addition, the 'functions' of teaching, training, pastoring and missioning are monitored by *panels.*

As an example, let us consider the functions of teaching and training. Each programme committee designates one of its members to be its 'T 'n T' supervisor. This person assesses learning needs in that programme and develops an appropriate curriculum, which may range from a set of simple devotional resources for use in family networks to a systematic course on basic beliefs offered in the youth programme at a certain time in the year. Periodically (maybe three times annually), all the 'T 'n T' supervisors from the various committees sit down together with the theological staff to examine the life of the church from the point of view of equipping the members for 'every good work' (2 Tim 3:17). They are not concerned that study and training of many kinds is going on throughout the groups, for we don't all come out of the same mould! But they are concerned (a) to ensure that one way or another every member is acquiring a basic understanding of the Bible; (b) the teaching is 'sound' (in the sense intended by 2 Tim 3:3); (c) unhelpful overlap is being minimised; and (d) adequate leadership and resources are being provided. Periodically the group surveys congregational needs with instruments such as the Needs Assessment Questionnaire featured in chapter six.

The pastoral panel consists similarly of the pastoral supervisors from each programme committee. On their committees, these people are concerned to ensure that every participant in the programme has some connection with a small caring group and a pastoral relationship with some church leader. On the panel, they review the names of each person in the whole church flock, ensuring that none is overlooked or, by virtue of participation in several programmes, overwhelmed with well-intentioned visitations!

The mission panel is concerned to guard the programme committees against an inward-looking concern for their own edification, and claims on the time of their members so heavy, that the call to mission is neglected. Opportunities to turn learning into service and witness are constantly sought. Outreach, personal evangelism, social services, family counselling, public activism and missionary support are all ways in which faith becomes manifest in good works. Sometimes a particular programme will aspire to sponsor a special mission project on a fairly large scale, and there is then a need to ensure that it fits in with the general target-priorities of the congregation as a whole and does not place too heavy demands on just a few. That is where the exchange of ideas on the panel is valuable.

It may turn out that some special projects are of long duration and require skilled support back-up. Examples might be the running of a child-care centre, an evangelistic communications unit, a crisis counselling and accommodation bureau, a day-care centre for the elderly, or a church-based community support scheme for unemployed youth. A separate committee is shown in the diagram which operates to co-ordinate congregational support and prayer for these projects, and to see that they are given adequate resources and administrative back-up.

The lattice allows for expansion in other ways as well. It may be that several committees appoint music supervisors to draw out the musical talents of members and to build up a vocabulary of praise for each group. Such people could also come together as a panel to think both theologically and musically about the ministry of well-chosen songs and instrumental contributions. This is a further horizontal mechanism.

Another possibility is that the committee for adult programmes might see value in sub-dividing into more specialist divisions catering separately for, say, adults in middle life and others in the years of retirement. This is a further vertical mechanism. The structure is responsive to the needs of the body.

It is important to remember that the lattice, for all that it looks somewhat like a Heath Robinson contraption, is a facilitating structure, not a goal in itself. As the various committees fill up with real flesh-and-blood people, each with a task that is clearly and functionally defined, so the gifts of the Spirit nourish a living body. If every task identified on the lattice in diagram 9.5 were to be performed by a separate person, then something in excess of fifty people would be performing enabling ministries on behalf of those involved at the level called 'Action'.

From one point of view this sounds unnecessarily cumbersome. There are two justifications. First, such people are not merely sitting around on committees. The portfolios they bear are concerned with spiritual leadership, teaching, training, pastoring and other ministries of an enabling kind. Committee meetings are concerned with evaluation of what is going on with a view to planning and praying for individuals and outcomes. Secondly, bearing in mind that this model is meant to be serviceable for a church of a 'few hundreds', the involvement of so many in committee work is by no means excessive. Especially when committee work is so closely identified with ministry to persons.

Postscript

In developing the administrative lattice shown here, I have tried to avoid using names for the positions and structures depicted which are already familiar in various denominational structures, such as 'diaconates' and 'elders'. There were two reasons for this. One was to avoid importing into my diagram the extraneous connotations which some readers might attach to such terms. The other was to leave the door open for a church interested in modifying its procedures, along the lines suggested, to do so by revising the terms of reference of existing committees rather than by adding additional structures or abolishing familiar ones.

Nevertheless, I wish to express concern about a very common error in the operation of governing bodies in churches. The notion of 'elders' is usually linked at one and the same time with two quite different functions. One is the function of administrative leadership; the other is the function of interpersonal pastoral care. The gifts required for these respective roles are usually found in people of quite different personality types. Many churches, however, recruit people noted for their administrative abilities to their governing councils — which makes some sense — and then charge them to pastor several families as well. Conversely, some churches recruit people with pastoral gifts to committees which are to make decisions mainly affecting theological and administrative policy.

In our administrative lattice, the 'council of ministries' is the place where full-time staff and programme convenors confer on policy and co-ordination. Those with pastoral gifts come into their own elsewhere in the lattice. They could only be regarded as less important than those 'higher' in the structure by people who think, in the world's way, that persons who are named at the top of an administration flow-chart are more important than the activities and people referred to at the bottom. Christ was saying quite the opposite when he kneeled to wash the disciples' feet.

Core Curriculum

It was mentioned that the 'T 'n T' panel has a particular concern for the balance of teaching and training being provided through the church's various programmes. Is it reasonable to speak of a 'core curriculum' in this connection?

From time to time in general educational circles attempts are made to describe and justify the learning objectives and content which are considered to be obligatory for *all* students in compulsory education. Such attempts usually meet with great opposition because our modern, pluralistic societies are hard put to achieve agreement on the ends worth pursuing. It is, however, a quest to be encouraged, and one to which Christian people may reasonably be challenged to make a positive and persuasive contribution. In Australia, there has recently been an upsurge of debate on core curriculum as a result of a discussion booklet produced by the national Curriculum Development Centre.[16] This proposal includes belief systems and value stances as one of its nine major priority areas.

Is it feasible to think of a local church having a core curriculum? In churches where the main teaching input which members experience is the Sunday sermon, this in effect becomes the core curriculum for adults. Where one clergyman is mainly responsible for the use to which this time is put, there are risks that, lacking training in curriculum development, he may either preach to the preoccupation of the moment, thereby robbing the people of a sense of cumulative gains in their understanding of the faith, or follow a sequence that is logical in terms of his own experience but not keyed in to the needs of his members.

An increasing number of churches is bringing some sequence into their pulpit ministries by following *lectionaries*, i.e. calendars of biblical readings for public worship, designed to sample the Scriptures at varying levels of comprehensiveness, depending on whether they employ a cycle of one or more years' duration. It is impossible to keep theological bias out of a lectionary, except by doggedly determining to use every verse in the Bible for public reading, in strictly consecutive order. Even that says something about one's theological stance.

Some principles of selection are unavoidable, and the minimum pedagogic requirement of each passage selected is that it would be neither unreasonably long for the congregation's span of attention nor deprived of intelligibility when read by itself, independent of its surrounding context. Two other factors, having more theological roots, need to be taken into account in evaluating the usefulness of a particular lectionary.

One is the approach adopted towards the OT. The extreme possibilities are either to adhere doggedly to consecutive readings from Genesis to Malachi, or merely to pick out passages which support the main readings for the day from the NT. Or even to omit most of the OT except for a score or so 'purple' passages and some psalms. Somewhere between these extremes lies a selective principle which chooses passages comprehensively representative of the whole, moving by sequential reading along a path which exemplified both the progressive and the ever-contemporary aspects of the OT revelation. A recent book by Graeme Goldsworthy, *Gospel and Kingdom*,[17] masterfully defines the proper place of the OT record in the Christian's thought and experience in a style very useful for teachers and preachers in their preparation.

The second factor is the degree to which consecutive Bible teaching is sub-ordinated to readings representing themes of the traditional church year. Some lectionaries take such care to accommodate major feasts and saints' days that the learning outcome is likely to be a greater reliance on the authority of the church and its tradition than on the plain teaching of Scripture.

The Australian lectionary, published in 1978 by the Anglican Church of Australia, is a revision of the three-year cycle launched after the Second Vatican Council by the Roman Catholic Church, and several other denominations have adopted it as well. The full lectionary provides a reading from the Psalms, the OT and the NT for each day. The Uniting Church has issued an adaptation providing a Psalm, OT, Gospel and other NT reading for each Sunday, using the Gospel reading to establish the theme for the others. There are occasional sequences which allow for consecutive attention to particular epistles, but the OT selections roam capriciously from week to week, and ecclesiastical rather than expository motives dominate the rest. As a teaching aid, the Australian Lectionary is likely to cause some frustration to churches favouring sequential biblical exposition, but it is much to be preferred to the *ad hoc* caprice of preachers who have no developing plan of teaching.

A further step towards relevant core teaching in the weekly large-group worship is to establish a committee to plan and evaluate continuously this particular body-life activity as shown in the administrative lattice. Such a committee would help the preachers, clerical and lay, to work for cumulative learning over the long haul, integrating it with the other activities of prayer, praise and music into purposeful worship experiences. It would regularly sample congregational reactions to various aspects of the weekly service and in particular monitor the effectiveness of the teaching segment.

Nevertheless, as was suggested in the previous chapter, the effect of sole dependence on this avenue of teaching to develop the core understanding of the faith would be relatively superficial. Both young and old vary greatly as to the point each person has reached in the great pilgrimage, and smaller groups working through systematic study materials, allied to constant encouragement to members to be daily students of the Bible using some systematic calendar, such as that marketed internationally by the Scripture Union, are more effective ways to guarantee that individual members will become well-grounded in a faith they understand and apply to life.

The Church Calendar

Essential to the success of the administrative structures suggested above is a pre-planned schedule of meeting times and activities. Where dates of committee meetings are not laid out well in advance, people tend either to slip into the syndrome of monthly meetings without justification, or to feel over-involved and put upon when asked to negotiate the date of the next meeting at short notice. It is no restriction of the free movement of the Spirit of God to lay down a ground-plan for the year. People are able to gauge their level of real involvement from this. By entering dates into their diaries months ahead they can keep a check on what their cumulative commitments are and avoid the absences which erode their effectiveness. It is easier to cancel meetings which appear to be unnecessary than at the last moment to convene meetings which *are* needed.

Another advantage of a pre-planned schedule, especially when some committees are planned to meet infrequently, is that those committees or panels which are required to report to other bodies, such as the committee of ministries, can be scheduled to meet at a convenient interval of time *before* the 'higher' body meets. Too far apart, and time for action is delayed; too close, and reports won't be ready in time to go out with the agenda for the meeting of the higher body.

Epilogue

It may appear that in this last chapter I have exceeded my brief and moved outside a consideration of the church's teaching ministries to consider higher matters of churchmanship and policy. I offer two justifications.

First, I have maintained throughout this book that the teaching ministries within the faith-community are not self-sustaining ends in themselves, but means towards *each* of the goals which that community considers important. Hence it was necessary to engage in a certain amount of discussion as to what the Scripture indicates those goals should be, and to do that involved asking why God has raised up churches.

Secondly, I have also maintained that a proper placement of the ministry of teaching in the church depends on our recognising that the kind of teaching we are talking about requires a gift of the Spirit. Therefore we needed to explore what part spiritual gifts should play in the life of the church. The answer so clearly brought the lay people, so called, right into the active ministries of the church that we were obliged to spell out two major implications.

The first was the need to ally teaching with training at all levels. A learning church is learning not only the gospel but 'gospelling'. The second was the need to re-examine traditional organisational structures, particularly from the point of view of their adequacy or inefficiency as learning environments. They may also be judged on other criteria, such as their compatibility with Christian interpersonal values, their plausibility in the present cultural setting, and so on. But purely on this one criteria of their usefulness as learning environments, our enquiry caused us to raise many questions about current church structures.

The critical reader may choose to point out that it was not for the author, a layman in the ecclesiastical sense, to meddle with such matters. But I am unrepentant about my excursion into ecclesiology, for it has not only confirmed my belief that we are all *lay* persons, that is, the people of God (Gk: *laòs theoû*), but it has opened up the reservoir of gifts which the Spirit is longing to release in greater measure on the church and in the world. In the task of identifying and developing these gifts, those with the enabling gift of teaching are meant to be playing a crucial part. It is my hope that this book will have assisted them to understand better the dimensions of that holy task.

Footnotes

1. J. Stott, *One People* (London: Falcon, 1969) 22–25.
2. *Ibid.*, 21.
3. Act 1. See also Illich, *Deschooling*, and *Medical Nemesis* (London: Marion Boyars, 1975).
4. J. Price, ed., *Dialogues of Alfred North Whitehead* (New York: Mentor, 1954) 126.
5. Snyder, *Community*, 76.
6. *Ibid.*
7. *Ibid.*, 81.
8. Two words are commonly translated 'gifts'. *Dorēa* is the ordinary term as we use it today. *Charisma* represents the special grace-gifts conferred by the Holy Spirit. The present discussion is concerned with passages emphasising the second sense, including Ephesians 4, though the reference to 'gifts' in verse 8 of that chapter happens to be *dorata*, since it is quoting Psalm 68:18.
9. See Example 1, Part B.
10. The Greek word is *kubernēsis*, from which we obtain our word 'governor'. The related verb means to steer, and also relates to *kubernētēs*, used for the steersman or pilot in Acts 27:11.
11. The verb captures the true sense of *ekklēsia*, which refers not to a structured organisation but to the practice of congregating or assembling.

12. I trust the reader will forgive the repetition. One feature of good teaching is reinforcement by the repetition of main ideas!
13. See chapter four.
14. Do you agree? A fifth of a tenth is a fiftieth. Multiply by fifty is one equivalent salary. This, of course, is taking the word 'tithe' literally. Another argument generating the same figure is to invite people to commit two cents in every dollar they earn.
15. Snyder, *Community*, 123.
16. *Core Curriculum for Australian Schools* (Canberra: Curriculum Development Centre, 1980).
17. G. Goldsworthy, *Gospel and Kingdom* (Exeter: Paternoster, 1982). For further reading in the same vein, see Goldsworthy, *The Gospel in Revelation* (1984) and W.J. Dumbrell, *Covenant and Creation* (1984) and *The End of the Beginning* (forthcoming 1985), all published by Lancer Books, Sydney.

Select Bibliography

A. BOOKS

Banks, R. *Paul's Idea of Community*, Sydney: Lancer, 1980.
Barclay, W. *Educational Ideals in the Ancient World*, Grand Rapids: Baker, 1974.
Bowles, S. and Gintis, R. *Schooling in Capitalist America*, London: Routledge and Kegan Paul, 1976.
Boyd, W. and King, E.J. *The History of Western Education*, London: Adam and Charles Black, 10th ed., 1972.
Brown, L. and W. *The Christian Family*, New York: Association, 1959.
Brubacher, J.S. *A History of the Problems of Education*, New York: McGraw-Hill, 2nd ed., 1966.
Buber, M. *I and Thou*, trans. R.G. Smith, New York: Scribners, 2nd ed., 1958.
Buckland, R. *Children of the King*, Sydney: Anzea, 1979.
Bushnell, H. *Christian Nurture*, Grand Rapids: Baker, 1979.
Collins, C.W. and Hughes, P. *Where are Our Junior Secondary Schools Heading?*, Melbourne: ACER, 1982.
Cox, A.I. *Christian Education in the Church Today*, Nashville: Graded, 1965.
Cox, C.E. *Changing Aims in Religious Education*, London: Routledge and Kegan Paul, 1966.
Cox, H. *The Secular City*, Harmondsworth: Penguin, 1968.
Cully, I.V. and Brubaker Cully, K. eds, *Process and Relationship: Issues in Theory, Philosophy, and Religious Education*, Birmingham: Religious Education, 1978.
Cummings, D.B. ed, *The Purpose of Christ-centred Education*, Phillipsburg: Presbyterian and Reformed, 1979.
Curriculum Development Centre, *Core Curriculum for Australian Schools*, Canberra: CDC, 1980.
Davies, R.E. *An Approach to Christian Education*, London: Epworth, 1957.
d'Cruz, J.V. and Sheehan, P.J. eds, *Concepts of Education*, Melbourne: Dove, 1976.
Dobson, J. *Hide or Seek*, Old Tappan: Revell, 1974.
Eavey, C.B. *History of Christian Education*, Chicago: Moody, 1964.
Freire, P. *Pedagogy of the Oppressed*, trans. M.B. Ramos, London: Herder and Herder, 1970.
Fuller, E. *The Christian Idea of Education*, New Haven: Yale University, 1957.
Gangel, K.O. and Benson, W.S. *Christian Education: Its History and Philosophy*, Chicago: Moody, 1983.
Goldby, M. ed, *Curriculum Design*, London: Croom Helm, 1975.
Goldman, R. *Readiness for Religion*, London: Routledge and Kegan Paul, 1965.
———. *Religious Thinking from Childhood to Adolescence*, London: Routledge and Kegan Paul, 1964.
Goldsworthy, G. *Gospel and Kingdom*, Exeter: Paternoster, 1981.

Greaves, R.L. *The Puritan Revolution and Educational Thought*, New Brunswick: Rutgers University, 1969.
Groome, T.H. *Christian Religious Education*, Melbourne: Dove, 1980.
Hakes, J.E. ed, *An Introduction to Evangelical Christian Education*, Chicago: Moody, 1964.
Hengel, M. *Judaism and Hellenism*, trans. John Bowden, Philadelphia: Fortress, one-vol. ed, 1981.
Heynen, R. *The Christian Home*, Grand Rapids, Mich: Baker Book House, 1975.
Hill, B.V. ed, *A Charge to Keep*, Sydney: Aldersgate Fellowship, 1971.
Hill, B.V. *A Teenager is Many People*, Sydney: Anzea, 1970.
———. *Called to Teach*, Sydney: Angus and Robertson, 1971.
———. *Education and the Endangered Individual*, New York: Teachers College, 1973.
———. *Faith at the Blackboard*, Grand Rapids: Eerdmans, 1982.
Hirst, P.H. *Knowledge and the Curriculum*, London: Routledge and Kegan Paul, 1975.
Hirst, P.H. and Peters, R.S. *The Logic of Education*, London: Routledge and Kegan Paul, 1970.
Holley, R. *Religious Education and Religious Understanding*, London: Routledge and Kegan Paul, 1978.
Howe, R. *Man's Need and God's Action*, New York: Seabury, 1953.
Hull, J.M. *School Worship: An Obituary*, London: SCM, 1975.
Hyde, K.E. *Religious Learning in Adolescence*, Edinburgh: Oliver and Boyd, 1965.
Illich, I. *Deschooling Society*, New York: Harper and Row, 1970.
———. *Medical Nemesis*, London: Marion Boyars, 1975.
Jarman, T.L. *Landmarks in the History of Education*, London: John Murray, 2nd ed, 1970.
Knowles, M.S. *The Modern Practice of Adult Education*, New York: Association, 1970.
Laqueur, T.W. *Religion and Respectability: Sunday Schools and Working Class Culture; 1780–1850*, New Haven: Yale University, 1976.
Lewis, C.S. *Christian Reflections*, London: Geoffrey Bles, 1967.
Lister, I. *Deschooling: A Reader*, Cambridge: Cambridge University, 1971.
Loukes, H. *Teenage Religion*, London: SCM, 1961.
Magee, J. *Reality and Prayer*, London: Hodder and Stoughton, 1958.
Mager, R.F. *Preparing Instructional Objectives*, Belmont: Fearon, 1962.
Mallison, J. *The Small Group Book Series*, Sydney: Renewal, 1976.
Martin, R.P. *Worship in the Early Church*, Grand Rapids: Eerdmans, 1978.
Mathews, H.F. *Revolution in Religious Education*, Oxford: Religious Education, 1966.
McNeil, J.D. *Curriculum*, Boston: Little, Brown and Co, 1977.
Narramore, B. *Guide to Child Rearing*, Grand Rapids: Zondervan, 1972.
———. *Help! I'm a Parent*, Grand Rapids: Zondervan, 1972.
Nelson, C.E. *Where Faith Begins*, Atlanta: John Knox, 1976.
Pearson, K. and Allsop, I. eds, *Family Activities: A Collection of Resources for Intergenerational Groups*, Melbourne: Joint Board of Christian Education, 1977.
Phillips, J.B. *Ring of Truth*, London: Hodder and Stoughton, 1967.
Pollock, J.C. *The Good Seed*, London: Hodder and Stoughton, 1959.
Pounds, R.L. *The Development of Education in Western Culture*, New York: Appleton-Century-Crofts, 1968.
Prince, J.R. *Tuned in to Change*, Sydney: Anzea, 1981.
Purnell, D. *Working with Families*, Melbourne: Joint Board of Christian Education, 1980.
Richards, L.O. *Creative Bible Teaching*, Chicago: Moody, 1970.
———. *A Theology of Christian Education*, Grand Rapids: Zondervan, 1975.
Richardson, A. *The Bible in the Age of Science*, London: SCM, 1961.

Rossiter, G.R. *Religious Education in Australian Schools*, Canberra: Curriculum Development Centre, 1982.
Rummery, R.M. *Catechesis and Religious Education in a Pluralist Society*, Sydney: Dwyer, 1975.
Sanner, A.E. and A.F. Harper eds, *Exploring Christian Education*, Grand Rapids: Baker, 1978.
Shinn, R. *The Educational Mission of Our Church*, Boston: United Church, 1962.
Smith, V. *Alternatives in Education*, Bloomington: Phi Delta Kappa, 1976.
Snook, I.A. ed, *Concepts of Indoctrination*, London: Routledge and Kegan Paul, 1972.
Snyder, H.A. *The Community of the King*, Downers Grove: IVP, 1978.
———. *Liberating the Church*, Basingstoke: Marshall, Morgan and Scott, 1983.
Stedman, R. *Body Life*, Glendale: Regal, 2nd ed, 1977.
Stott, J. *One People*, London: Falcon, 1969.
Swomley, J.M. Jr. *Religion, The State and The Schools*, New York: Pegasus, 1968.
Taba, H. *Curriculum Development: Theory and Practice*, New York: Harcourt Brace and World, 1962.
Taylor, M.J. ed, *An Introduction to Christian Education*, Nashville: Abingdon, 1966.
Thiselton, A. *The Two Horizons*, Exeter: Paternoster, 1979.
Trigg, R. *Reason and Commitment*, Cambridge: Cambridge University, 1973.
Tyler, R.W. *Basic Principles of Curriculum and Instruction*, Chicago: University of Chicago, 1971.
Walker, W. *A History of the Christian Church*, Edinburgh: T. and T. Clark, 1918.
Wardle, D. *The Rise of the Schooled Society*, London: Routledge and Kegan Paul, 1974.
Westerhoff, J.H. III. and Neville, G.K. *Generation to Generation*, New York: Pilgrim, 1974.
Westerhoff, J.H. III. *Who are We? The Quest for a Religious Education*, Birmingham, Ala: Religious Education, 1979.
———. *Will Our Children Have Faith?* New York: Seabury, 1976.
Williamson, W.B. *Language and Concepts in Christian Education*, Philadelphia: Westminster, 1970.
Winter, D. *For All the People*, London: Hodder and Stoughton, 1967.

B. ARTICLES

Andersen, W.E. 'The Christian Conception of Maturity,' *JCE* 3:3 (1960) 142–52 and 4:1 and 2 (1961) 37–46 and 94–103.
Giles, K.N. 'Teachers and Teaching in the Church,' *JCE* 70 (April, 1981) 5–17.
Hill, B.V. 'Compulsion in Education,' *JCE* 52 (August, 1952) 39–57.
———. 'Education for Commitment: A Logical Contradiction?,' *JET* 15 (December, 1981) 159–70.
———. 'Is it Time We Deschooled Christianity?,' *JCE* 63 (November, 1978) 5–21.
———. 'Religious Instruction: An Anachronism?,' *JCE* 50 (October, 1974) 35–45.
———. "What's 'Open' About Open Education?" in *The Philosophy of Open Education*, ed. D. Nyberg; London: Routledge and Kegan Paul, 1975, 3–13.
Judge, E.A. 'The Conflict of Educational Aims in New Testament Thought,' *JCE* 9 (June, 1966) 32–45.
Kleinig, J. 'Educating and Indoctrinating,' in *Concepts of Education*, ed. J.V. d'Cruz and P.J. Sheehan; Melbourne: Dove, 1976, 23–31.

Niebuhr, Reinhold, 'The Two Sources of Western Culture,' in *The Christian Idea of Education*, ed. Edmund Fuller; New Haven: Yale University, 1957, 237–54.
Padilla, C.R. 'The Interpreted Word: Reflections on Contextual Hermeneutics,' *Them* 7 (September, 1981) 18–23.
Vose, G.N. 'The Puritans and Education: A Plea for Reassessment,' *JCE* 3 (December, 1960) 109–18.
White, R. 'The School in Calvin's Thought and Practice,' *JCE* 12 (June, 1969) 3–26.
Wise, F.F. 'The Family,' in *Exploring Christian Education*, ed. A.E. Sanner and A.F. Harper; Grand Rapids: Baker, 1978, 148–51.
Wynn, J.C. 'The Home and Christian Education,' in *An Introduction to Christian Education*, ed. M.J. Taylor; Nashville: Abingdon, 1966, 292–301.